Linux Desktop
Pocket Guide

Linux Desktop
Pocket Guide

David Brickner

O'REILLY®

Beijing · Cambridge · Farnham · Köln · Paris · Sebastopol · Taipei · Tokyo

Linux Desktop Pocket Guide

by David Brickner

Copyright © 2005 O'Reilly Media, Inc. All rights reserved.
Printed in the United States of America.

Published by O'Reilly Media, Inc., 1005 Gravenstein Highway North, Sebastopol, CA 95472.

O'Reilly books may be purchased for educational, business, or sales promotional use. Online editions are also available for most titles (*safari.oreilly.com*). For more information, contact our corporate/ institutional sales department: (800) 998-9938 or *corporate@oreilly.com*.

Editor:	David Brickner
Production Editor:	Marlowe Shaeffer
Cover Designer:	Emma Colby
Interior Designer:	David Futato

Printing History:

September 2005:   First Edition.

0-596-10104-X
[C]

Contents

Preface

Linux has always been a desktop operating system. This was true when Linus Torvalds created it on his personal computer in 1991, and it remains true today for the millions of people who use it as their daily desktop or laptop OS.

This book is a short guide to help you get the most out of your desktop Linux experience. Instead of focusing upon the commands you can run in a shell, as the *Linux Pocket Guide* (O'Reilly) does, this reference is about the graphical programs and desktop environments that run on top of Linux. Here you'll find out which programs are the best in their respective categories, what features those programs have, and where to get them.

Although using Linux is usually very easy, there are some sticking points where even experienced Linux users may have a hard time. Almost all of these are related to getting Linux to work perfectly with hardware. This book doesn't shy away from these sometimes difficult topics, and it jumps right in and tells you what you need to know about laptop power management, configuring your graphics card, and setting up sound and networking. No matter how good Linux desktop programs are, you'll never be satisfied with them until your hardware works as it should.

Though it is impossible for such a small book to be exhaustive, I'm going to tackle the ambitious goal of providing information that is helpful to users of five of the most popular Linux distributions: Fedora, Gentoo, Mandriva (formerly known as Mandrake), Novell SUSE, and the desktop-focused Debian derivative Ubuntu.

What Is Linux?

If you've bought this book, you probably already know the answer to this question. But just in case you're in the store and your purchase decision hinges on being told what Linux is, here goes.

Linux is an operating system like Microsoft Windows and Mac OS X. You can run Linux in place of those operating systems, on the same hardware, which is what millions of people do everyday. Linux was created by Linus Torvalds in 1991 when he was in college, but it has since been improved upon by thousands of programmers around the world.

Linux is what is known as Free Software. The programming code that makes up Linux is licensed such that everyone has the freedom to run, copy, distribute, study, change, and improve the software—thus the term "free." The free nature of Linux is what has allowed so many other programmers to improve Linux and is essential to its continued growth. To learn more about Free Software, visit *http://www.fsf.org*.

Although you can't run most Windows programs on Linux, you'll find no shortage of alternative, free programs that perform similar functions. Many popular applications, such as the Firefox web browser, Thunderbird email client, and OpenOffice.org office suite are cross-platform and run equally well on Windows and Linux. This book introduces you to several of these programs.

The Linux operating system is highly modular and is comprised of components that build on top of each other to provide a complete computing experience. Understanding this building-block nature may help you better understand the components that I discuss later in the book. Here is one way to break down the Linux OS:

Linux kernel

Linux is a both a generic name applied to the operating system and the specific name of one component of that OS, the *kernel*. A kernel is the core of the OS. It handles interaction with the hardware of the computer. This book deals with the kernel only when necessary—for example, to help you configure a piece of hardware (like a sound or video card) or configure power management on a laptop.

Utilities and libraries

The kernel by itself isn't particularly useful without additional programs and utilities. Many of these are provided by the GNU project;* so many, in fact, that some people hold these utilities to be of equal importance with the kernel and believe the combined OS should be called GNU/Linux. This book is not focused on these utilities, but it will mention some in pursuit of performing a larger task, like prolonging laptop battery life.

Shell

Also known as the command line, this is an alternative interface to Linux that is entirely text-based. Don't be dismissive of it because it looks like DOS from the 1980s—it is much more powerful than that. From time to time, I'll ask you to perform a task at the command line, as it is sometimes the simplest or even the only way to get the job done. The Appendix provides a very brief introduction to the command line.

X

As I just pointed out, Linux can be run without any type of graphical user interface (GUI). This is very useful when running Linux on a server because system resources don't have to be devoted to running a GUI

---

* The GNU project was started by Richard Stallman in 1984 with the goal of building a free Unix-style operating system. GNU is a recursive acronym that stands for "GNU's Not Unix" and it is pronounced "guh-noo."

(and it is one less thing to crash or have security issues). But for a desktop, a GUI is essential, and X is the underlying technology that makes a GUI possible. Its function is to control how shapes and colors are drawn on the screen, but it does not control the visual appearance of those shapes—this is a task left for window managers (see the next entry in this list). X also controls your display, keyboard, mice, and, to some extent, your fonts; the section "X," in Chapter 7, helps you configure these devices.

Window managers and desktop environments

These run on top of X and give you a pretty GUI to work with. Window managers provide just the basics—windows with borders that you can drag around and resize. Desktop environments (GNOME and KDE are the big two) provide a lot more, such as taskbars, file managers, menus, icons, and control panels. This is what most users think of as the operating system, and it's where you'll spend most of your time while using Linux. I cover both of these desktop environments later in the book. In practice, the line between window managers and desktop environments can sometimes be blurry, but it really isn't an important distinction for most users.

Applications

Linux has thousands of applications. Some are text-only and are designed to be run at a command line; others are graphical programs meant to be run on X. Chapter 5 is devoted to introducing many common applications that you can run on Linux.

Linux is under constant development. There are improvements to applications and utilities on a daily basis, and core programs like X or the desktop environments are updated every six months or so, adding significant improvements in stability, security, and features. And the best part is that these updates are available to you at no extra charge.

Missing Screenshots and the Command Line

As you flip through this book, one of the questions you might ask is, "Where are all the screenshots?" The answer is that there aren't any. I do realize this is a desktop book, and it is mostly about graphical applications, but, in the end, I just didn't see the need to fill the book with screenshots. If you want to see how a program looks, visit the program's main web site, which I've tried to always provide a link to, and look at the images there in large format and full color. Trust me: screenshots in a pocket reference can't even begin to do a program justice. Besides, they would have just taken up the space that I'd rather use to explain another cool feature of KDE or to provide one more tip for managing your programs.

The second question you may ask is, "What are all these commands you want me to type?" The answer is that using Linux on the desktop still means you should know how to use the command line and configure a program by editing a text file. Linux simply doesn't have all the graphical tools necessary to configure every possible setting in the thousands of programs it supports. And you know what—I'm glad it doesn't. Though I used to fear the command line and dread the thought of using *vi* to edit an X configuration file, I've since learned that the command line is often the simplest and fastest way to get something useful done.

The only reason Windows users don't think of the command line as one of the most useful parts of a desktop operating system is merely because Windows has such a crappy command line. Linux doesn't. What you can do at the command line—and the ease with which you can do it (once you know the right command)—is a *feature*.

In an attempt to make this book as standalone as possible, I've provided an appendix that gives you the very basics of using the command line, including making edits to text files.

Conventions Used in This Book

The following is a list of the typographical conventions used in this book:

Italic

> Used to indicate URLs, filenames, filename extensions, and directory/folder names. For example, a path in the filesystem will appear as */Developer/Applications*.

`Constant width`

> Used to show code examples, the contents of files, and console output, as well as the names of variables, commands, and other code excerpts.

`Constant-width bold`

> Used to display commands or text that the user should type directly.

`Constant-width italic`

> Used in code examples and tables to show sample text to be replaced with your own values.

You should pay special attention to notes set apart from the text with the following styles:

TIP

This is a tip, suggestion, or general note. It contains useful supplementary information about the topic at hand.

WARNING

This is a warning or note of caution.

How to Contact Us

We have tested and verified the information in this book to the best of our ability, but you may find that features have changed (or even that we have made mistakes!). As a reader of this book, you can help us to improve future editions by sending us your feedback. Please let us know about any errors, inaccuracies, bugs, misleading or confusing statements, and typos that you find anywhere in this book.

Please also let us know what we can do to make this book more useful to you. We take your comments seriously and will try to incorporate reasonable suggestions into future editions. You can write to us at:

O'Reilly Media, Inc.
1005 Gravenstein Hwy N.
Sebastopol, CA 95472
(800) 998-9938 (in the U.S. or Canada)
(707) 829-0515 (international/local)
(707) 829-0104 (fax)

To ask technical questions or to comment on the book, send email to:

bookquestions@oreilly.com

The web site for *Linux Desktop Pocket Guide* lists examples, errata, and plans for future editions. You can find this page at:

http://www.oreilly.com/catalog/linuxdesktoppr

For more information about this book and others, see the O'Reilly web site:

http://www.oreilly.com

Acknowledgments

As with my first book, *Test Driving Linux*, this one would not have been possible without the support of my wife. She really kept me motivated throughout the project and gave me the determination to see it through. I never would have thought writing a "tiny" pocket guide could possibly take so long.

I also thank Keith Fahlgren for reading through the book and making helpful suggestions.

This book would not be possible without the hard work put into it by the O'Reilly production staff. Marlowe Shaeffer was the production editor and proofreader for the book, Nancy Kotary copyedited, and Judy Hoer did her usual excellent job on the index. The cover design was by Emma Colby, one of her last before moving on from O'Reilly.

This book is dedicated to my father. I wish I knew back in 1984 what a gift you were giving me by allowing me time to play games on your new computer. Thank you for all of the support you have given me throughout my life.

## CHAPTER 1

Distributions

As I explained in the Preface, Linux is really just the core of an operating system, not particularly useful for your desktop by itself. The other components that make it a usable OS are developed by thousands of individuals and groups. Because there is no single point of control exerted on the entire OS, as Microsoft exerts on Windows and Apple on Mac OS X, there is no "definitive" Linux operating system. Instead, individuals, groups, and businesses package the different open source components together, add a few unique programs (installers, configuration programs, and artwork), and call the result a Linux *distribution*.

There are hundreds of Linux distributions that you can use as your desktop operating system. Choosing from among them can be a difficult task, particularly when you are new to Linux and don't know the distinguishing characteristics of each distribution. If you aren't experienced with Linux or haven't yet branched out beyond your first distribution, I hope you'll find this chapter a valuable introduction to the popular distributions.

Choosing a Distribution

The good news is that Linux distributions are more alike than they are different. They are all stable, fast, and secure, and they run the same web browsers, email clients, and desktop environments. Once installed, you can get most any distribution to do what any other distribution can do. What makes each distribution truly different is the path it takes to get you there. Some will be difficult to install but very easy to configure afterwards; some have almost nonexistent documentation but are so simple to keep up-to-date that you might not need any. After using Linux on the desktop for six years and trying more than a dozen distributions, I've identified four broad factors that you can use to compare distributions; these factors will help you determine which distribution may be most appropriate for your skill level and needs. These are:

Installation

I define "installation" as the act of getting Linux placed upon your hard drive and getting your system to boot. Most distributions provide equally capable installation programs. You typically install the distribution only once per machine, so this isn't as important as many people would have you believe. However, the better the installation routine of a distribution is, the more you'll enjoy your first interaction with the system, and, more importantly, the less work there is to do to completely configure the system afterwards.

Configuration

Configuration is when you make sure your network, sound, and video cards are fully working; when your peripherals are attached and operational; and when your user environment is set up the way you want. Technically, configuration never ends, but most people consider it to be at an end once they have all of their hardware configured. The ease of configuration is where many distributions distinguish themselves.

Program installation and upgrade

Another way that a distribution distinguishes itself is by the ease with which you can install new programs or update or remove exiting ones. This is typically called "package management." Although many distributions share a common package format, how well it works in practice can vary dramatically.

Documentation and community

While using Linux, you will occasionally have problems; in this regard, it is no different than using Windows XP or Mac OS X. Your ability to solve these problems is directly related to how much you already know, the quality of available documentation (both on the Web and in print), and the willingness of the distribution's community to help out. Good documentation and a friendly, knowledgeable community go a long way toward making up for weaknesses in other areas.

Table 1-1 ranks the five distributions discussed in this book using the four criteria I just mentioned. Keep in mind that these are my numbers only, based upon personal experience. I weight each category to show how important I regard it with relation to the others.

Table 1-1. Weighted comparison of five popular distributions

Item	Fedora	Gentoo	Mandriva	SUSE	Ubuntu
Installation (15%)	4	2	4	4	3
Configuration (25%)	3	3	4	4	3
Program installation (30%)	4	4	4	3[a]	5
Documentation (30%)	3	5	3	3[b]	4
Weighted average	3.45	3.75	3.70	3.40	3.90

[a] Despite the general excellence of the YaST program installation tool, I gave SUSE a slightly lower score than other RPM-based distributions because it does not provide a capable command-line variant.

[b] The boxed set of SUSE comes with a couple of excellent books, and the same documentation is available from within SUSE as online help. Though good, this documentation is not as helpful for troubleshooting and system configuration as a dynamic online community—thus the average score.

As you can see, the distributions are fairly close to each other when all the factors are considered. My suggestion is to start with a distribution that ranks high in installation and configuration first (such as Mandriva or SUSE). Get your toes wet. If you're ever ready to move on, the knowledge you gained from using this "easy" distribution will prove valuable when working with one that's slightly harder to install, but more forgiving or informative with regard to the last two criteria.

Though understanding the relative strengths of distributions can aid you in deciding which one to use, it might not be your only concern. For example, you might want a distribution that uses a particular package management scheme, one that has a GUI installer, one that lets you resize a Windows partition during installation, or one that supports your processor's architecture. Table 1-2 allows you to easily compare features across distributions. To compare an even broader range of distributions, see their respective pages at *http:// www.distrowatch.com*.

Table 1-2. Feature comparison across distributions

Criteria	Fedora	Gentoo	Mandriva	SUSE	Ubuntu
Processor architecture	i386,[a] x86-64, PPC, SPARC	x86,[b] x86-64, PPC, SPARC	i586,[c] x86-64, PPC	i586, x86-64	i386, x86-64, PPC
Package format	RPM	Source	RPM	RPM	Debian package
Package manager	Yum and apt-rpm	portage	urpmi and apt-rpm	YaST and apt-rpm	apt
GUI installer	Yes	No[d]	Yes	Yes	No[e]
Resize Windows partitions	No	No	Yes	Yes	No
Default desktop	GNOME	None	KDE	KDE	GNOME
# of CDs/DVDs	4/1	1	4/1	5/1	1

a i386-compiled distributions will run just fine on Pentium and higher processors but might not be as optimized as they could be.

b Gentoo allows you to specify exactly how you compile your system from the very beginning. It supports all probable variants of the x86 architecture and, if you choose, can be optimized for your specific processor architecture.

c i586-compiled distributions will not run on processors prior to Intel Pentium (x486 and x386). This is usually not a problem for most users.

d There is a beta graphical installer that may be usable by the time you read this.

e Though the installer is not GUI, it is menu-driven, which makes it quite simple to use and very fast.

The following sections provide detailed descriptions of each distribution covered in this book with respect to the four criteria laid out earlier in this section. The order is alphabetical.

Fedora

The Fedora project started in 2003 when Red Hat opened up their development process and created a community-driven distribution. This caused a lot of confusion at first, and many users didn't know if they should continue to track the commercial Red Hat releases, Fedora, or jump ship to an entirely new distribution. In the past two years, this confusion has largely cleared up and Fedora has become a respected and highly used Linux distribution. The main Fedora web site, found at *http://fedora.redhat.com*, contains documentation, release information, and links to download the distribution.

A new version of Fedora is released roughly every eight months. These are numbered releases starting with Fedora Core 1 up to the most recent, Fedora Core 4. Each new release updates core software—such as the kernel, GNOME, KDE, and X—and adds new features. As Red Hat uses Fedora as a testing ground for their commercial release, some of the new features or changes have a very "enterprise" feel to them, like the addition of Security Enhanced Linux (SELinux).

The default desktop for Fedora is GNOME. Although KDE can be installed, it is a heavily themed version that feels very different from the typical KDE install. In fact, if you like

KDE, I would say Fedora is a poor choice, unless you are prepared to install it from the source. However, the GNOME experience is one of the best, and I highly recommend Fedora if GNOME is your preferred desktop environment.

To avoid any legal hassles, the Fedora project follows the lead of Red Hat and doesn't include the necessary software to play DVDs, MP3s, or Windows Media files. The necessary support can be added easily once you configure a third-party package repository, as outlined in Chapter 6.

Installation

The installation program for Fedora is known as Anaconda; you will find this used as the installer for several other distributions, especially Red Hat derivatives. Though the installer asks several questions, none of them are particularly hard to answer. It does a decent job of detecting and setting up typical hardware, such as keyboards, mice, video cards, sound cards, and monitors. I've found it less capable at handling wireless cards, but, to be fair, many installers have this trouble. The installer can easily set up a dual-boot system (a system that can boot into either Windows or Linux), but it doesn't provide any support for resizing Windows partitions; this means you will need to use another tool to make room on your Windows hard drive for Fedora. What I like least about the installer is its linear nature, which makes it hard to jump back to earlier steps if you want to change a setting. Also, when installing Fedora Core 4, I ran into numerous errors when creating nondefault filesystems.

Configuration

Configuration of a Fedora system is a mix of distribution-specific utilities and configuration file editing. I've found the configuration programs to be capable, but not particularly fancy. Fedora has not yet developed a centralized control panel from which all of these tools can be accessed, which means that you'll need to choose the programs individually from the menu or run them from the command line. The good news is that Fedora's close relation to the commercially supported Red Hat means you'll often find that drivers and programs provided by third parties have a Fedora or Red Hat install package. Also, many commercial programs that are certified to run on Red Hat, such as Oracle, work with Fedora as well.

Package Management

Just like Red Hat, Fedora uses RPM files for package management. (RPM is a recursive acronym that means RPM Package Management, though at one point the R stood for Red Hat.) You can install RPMs from the command line or by using a GUI tool. RPMs perform a dependency check when you attempt to install them. This means they will tell you if you need to install other pieces of software on which the current program *depends*. Unfortunately, RPMs will not install the dependencies for you automatically or even locate them for you. This deficiency can be overcome by using a package manager such as Yum, which is the default package manager for Fedora and is covered in Chapter 6.

Documentation

A body of online documentation is slowly forming around Fedora in the form of Wikis, FAQs, and forums. There are more books published on Fedora than any other distribution, which may explain why the online documentation is taking so long to materialize. In many cases, I have often found it easiest to locate information on my particular problem by doing a web search, as opposed to visiting a specific site. This approach often didn't work well with Red Hat because a general web search frequently returned help for earlier versions of the software than what I was using, but because the Fedora name is new, almost all information I find on it is relevant to my particular problem. I've found two sites especially useful: the Unofficial Fedora FAQ (*http://www.fedorafaq.org*) and the forums (*http://www.fedoraforum.org*). The Fedora project maintains a page of other community resources, located at *http://fedora.redhat.com/participate/communicate/*.

Overall, I believe Fedora is a solid distribution that is great for beginners and experienced users alike. It is a particularly good choice if you are familiar with Red Hat server offerings, need to work with a distribution that is likely to be found in a business setting, or prefer GNOME and its related programs over KDE.

Gentoo

Gentoo (*http://www.gentoo.org*) is a fairly new distribution that began gaining popularity around 2002. Started by Daniel Robbins, it has since evolved into a very successful project that has captured the hearts of many Linux users. It is entirely free, so you don't need to purchase it from a web site or buy it in a store. There is a Gentoo store, however, where you can buy install CDs with nice artwork on them—such a purchase is an easy way to support the project.

The philosophy behind Gentoo is pretty much "Linux the way you want it." To this end, Gentoo is installed by compiling all of the programs from source—using a set of criteria known as USE flags, which you choose, and several compiler options to make the resulting programs run faster. This extreme configurability—and the tools to manage it—have helped to create an enthusiastic Gentoo fanbase. Some people liken Gentoo users to the car enthusiasts who put bolt-on performance parts on their cars; both groups seek extreme customization and performance.

In most cases, Gentoo doesn't favor one program over another, meaning that there are no default choices for the big questions like which web browser, desktop environment, or email client to use. This neutrality is different from many distributions that present you with a small set of default choices in order to provide a "better" experience. The choice is great, but when you don't like the defaults, and setting up the alternatives is difficult, you might find a distribution unusable. This is seldom the case with Gentoo, where—from the beginning—you can really have it your way.

One great thing about Gentoo is that you don't need to access third-party repositories in order to install software with full multimedia capabilities. However, you do need to pay attention to which USE flags you compile your software with in order to get all the features you are entitled to. The portage USE statement is fully explained in the portage documentation found at the Gentoo web site.

Installation

To install Gentoo, start by downloading one of the live CDs from the download link (appears as Get Gentoo!) on the main Gentoo page. You have the choice of downloading from an http or ftp mirror, or using BitTorrent. When you select the *mirror* link, you are taken to a list of mirror sites where you should choose one that is geographically close to you (but you might want to try others if your first selection is too slow). The mirror site link often takes you to a high-level Gentoo directory with several choices. To work with stable Gentoo releases, you should select the *release* link. Gentoo releases are named for the year and the release number. So, release 2005.1 is the second release in 2005 (the count starts at 0). Download the ISO image that corresponds with your processor architecture. There are three types of ISOs per architecture:

Minimal
> This live CD will boot your PC into a Gentoo environment where you can begin setting up your system. It is a minimal CD because it does not contain all the software

(known as *stages*) that you will need to complete your installation. Instead, the stages are downloaded as you need them.

Universal

This CD has all the functions of the minimal CD and includes all three software stages needed to complete the install. I recommend getting this CD in most cases, as you can reuse it on multiple machines without needing to download the later stages each time.

Package

This CD includes precompiled binaries of many software programs. This option is useful only if you are performing a GRP Gentoo install, which is when you use precompiled programs instead of building your own. The Gentoo documentation has more information about this type of install.

Although installing Gentoo requires running a lot of manual steps from the command line, the process is well-documented at the Gentoo web site and is not actually hard—just time-consuming. However, I do not recommend the process for someone who is not already familiar with Linux or who is not very comfortable with computers.

Configuration

As with the install, Gentoo does not hold your hand when it comes to configuring your system. There are no pretty GUI tools or centralized control panels, and very few command-line tools. What Gentoo does provide are sensible defaults, several well-commented configuration files, and an uncluttered feel that comes from not needing to support 10 years or more of legacy configuration methods. To configure a Gentoo system, you need to be comfortable editing configuration files and willing to dig for answers in the online documentation (more on that in a bit).

Package Management

Gemtoo's package management program is one of the two features that really sets it apart—the other is documentation. Known as *portage*, the program installer is a clever combination of Python and bash scripts (command-line scripts) that determines software dependencies, downloads all the required packages, and then compiles the software using compile-time settings that you choose. Using portage, you can easily install software that is optimized for your computer. The downside is that installing from source takes a long time, possibly a day or more, for large packages like KDE, OpenOffice.org, or X.org. Linux users who want the ultimate control over their software love the flexibility that portage gives them. If you're not willing to wait for your programs to compile, you can take advantage of the increasing number of precompiled programs available in portage. Of course, you lose the ability to customize the compile, which is one of the reasons for using Gentoo in the first place, but this is a nice way to try out a large program like OpenOffice.org without waiting for several hours.

Documentation

The Gentoo documentation and community are second to none (though new kid on the block Ubuntu is giving it a run). These two Gentoo "features"—package management and documentation—more than make up for the manual steps required to install and configure the distribution. Because Gentoo is only a few years old, both the documentation and the community are highly centralized. Almost all documents worth reading about Gentoo can be found at *http://www.gentoo.org/doc/en/index.xml*; support for your most vexing problems can be found at *http://forums.gentoo.org*. With these resources at your disposal, and an occasional visit to the Gentoo IRC channel #gentoo at irc.freenode.net, or the Gentoo Wiki at *http://gentoo-wiki.com/Main_Page*, there is almost no problem with Gentoo you cannot overcome.

I strongly recommend Gentoo as a desktop distribution for Linux hobbyists, computer enthusiasts, programmers, and system administrators. It really isn't the best distribution for those looking for a simple Linux experience, those with slow processors, or new Linux users.

Mandriva

Mandriva is the name of the distribution (and company) formed from the merger of the Mandrake and Connectiva distributions in early 2005. The effects of the merger are yet to be felt in the distribution itself, so you can largely consider the current release of Mandriva, known as LE for Limited Edition, to be equivalent to what would have been Mandrake 10.2. The main web site for Mandriva is *http://www.mandriva.com*.

Mandriva had one of the first truly easy-to-use graphical installers for Linux. This, combined with optimizations for Pentium processors (most distributions are compiled for x386 processors) and a tendency to include the latest versions of many programs, made Mandriva popular with enthusiasts, and earned it the reputation for being a good desktop distribution. All of this holds true today.

Traditionally, Mandriva has favored the KDE desktop over GNOME, but, for the past year or so, it has treated both almost equally. However, KDE is the default Mandriva desktop, it is usually more up-to-date than GNOME, and the appearance feels as if it has received just a bit more attention.

Refreshingly, Mandriva pulls out all the stops when it comes to enabling your computer to run all media types that Linux can support. Because of this, you don't need to install any additional software to watch DVDs, listen to MP3s, or playback Windows Media, QuickTime, or RealPlayer files.

You can obtain Mandriva in a variety of ways. It is available for sale from the Mandriva web site; you can join the Mandriva Club (*http://www.mandrivaclub.com*) to gain access to various downloads; or you can download the community versions of the software, known as download editions, from *http://www.mandrivalinux.com*. The downloadable editions do not include drivers or support for 3D graphics cards or playback of many media types. It is not difficult to add this support yourself, but if you want to avoid the hassle, get a paid-for version.

TIP

My first book *Test Driving Linux* (O'Reilly), details how to use the Mandriva Live CD known as *Move* to learn the Linux desktop. It is a useful guide for anyone using KDE and related applications, not only for Mandriva users.

Installation

As I mentioned earlier, Mandriva comes with a GUI installer that offers a nice blend of power and usability. One nice feature of this installer is its ability to resize existing Windows partitions to make room for Linux and set up your system to dual-boot. The installer does an adequate job with hardware detection and configuration, but it isn't perfect.

Configuration

One of the ways in which Mandriva has distinguished their distribution is in the area of configuration. There is a centralized control panel, known as the Mandrake* Control Center (accessible from Menu → Administer your system → Configure your computer), from which you can access several Mandriva-unique tools to fully configure the hardware on your system. The included tools help you set up your network,

---

* Maybe the name will be updated to Mandriva by the time you use it.

printer, monitor, hard disks and other storage devices, firewall, mouse and keyboard, and so on. Although this is not the only way to configure a Mandriva system, it is a great starting place for those who are reluctant to configure hardware and services from the command line.

Package Management

Mandriva is an RPM-based system like Fedora, but you usually can't use Fedora RPM packages on Mandriva. Mandriva has attempted to overcome the limitations of the RPM package format with a tool called *urpmi*, which not only checks for package dependencies, but downloads the required packages as well. Although a useful tool, it is still not as powerful as Gentoo's portage or Ubuntu's apt solutions; yet, it is significantly better than regular RPM tools. I've also had more difficulty removing programs with Mandriva than any other distribution. Sometimes the removal of a program—say, the Postfix email server—will require the removal of dozens more programs that shouldn't be affected at all, and that you may want to keep. This can be very frustrating when you are trying to remove unnecessary server software in order to run a lean desktop.

Documentation

Mandriva's documentation is no better than what you'll find for Fedora, but with the added disadvantage that there are no in-depth books written about it. Besides the scattering of information you'll find at distribution-agnostic web sites like *http://www.linuxquestions.org*, you'll find information in the forums found at *http://www.mandrivausers.org*, on personal web pages, and in the newsgroup *alt.os.mandrake*. Because of the sheer volume of Mandriva users (there are several millions of them), chances are good that you'll find some useful information through one of these resources.

If you need more help, consider signing up for the Mandriva Club, which is an online subscriber community with forums, FAQ, and direct access to some of the Mandriva developers. Indeed, Mandriva focuses a lot of attention on this community, as it is a significant source of revenue for the company. The web site is *http://www.mandrivaclub.com*.

Personally, I rather like Mandriva. Although I had been using Linux for a couple of years, Version 7.0 of Mandriva (called Mandrake back then) was the first distribution to give me a Linux desktop that I found really usable and enjoyable—and Mandriva has only gotten better. If you are new to Linux, Mandriva should be one of the first distributions you try.

SUSE

In the corporate world, SUSE is probably the second best known Linux distribution after Red Hat. Originally developed by the Germany company SUSE, LLC, it was purchased, in early 2004, by the American company Novell, which also purchased the Linux development house Ximian in 2003. These acquisitions show that Novell is placing its bets for future customers and growth on the popularity and technology of the Linux operating system. The future of the SUSE brand is uncertain, so by the time you read this book, the SUSE distribution may be called something else—such as Novell Linux or similar. Regardless, it is still the same technology, and what you read here should continue to apply. The main web site is *http://www.novell.com/linux/suse*. Pronunciation of SUSE varies, but, increasingly, you'll hear English speakers saying *sue-say*.

When thinking of SUSE, I can't help but compare it to German cars. Like a BMW or Mercedes, SUSE Linux is well-designed, well-engineered, powerful, and possesses a simple, understated elegance. Unlike pricey German cars, however, it is not any more expensive than other commercial Linux distributions.

Although pre-Novell SUSE favored the KDE desktop, post-Novell SUSE treats both desktop environments equally, which makes sense, considering that Ximian was a GNOME development shop. However, the default install and desktop is still KDE. No one knows how much longer this arrangement will continue, and there may come a day when one environment is clearly favored over the other. Until that time, enjoy the fact that, out of the box, SUSE offers the best KDE and GNOME experience of any commercial Linux distribution—in my opinion anyway.

Out of the box, SUSE's multimedia capabilities are not much better than Fedora's. You need to download support for many multimedia formats yourself (though SUSE makes them available through YaST—just look for the multimedia packs in the updates list). However, to play encrypted DVDs, you need to download the tools for a third-party repository, as outlined in Chapter 6.

You can purchase SUSE at retail stores, like CompUSA and Fry's, or you can order it from numerous sites on the Interent. The boxed set comes with two manuals: one for users and one for system administration. Both are excellent and are, hands-down, the best documentation you'll get with any Linux distribution. SUSE has never been as open as other distributions to making free downloads of the software available, and the situation hasn't changed under Novell management. To get SUSE cheaply, your best bet is to find a BitTorrent (check out *http://www.linuxISOtorrent.com*) or to order a copy from a discount site like *http://www.cheapbytes.com*.

Installation

SUSE comes with a powerful installation program known as YaST (Yet another Setup Tool). Its power comes from the sheer volume of settings that can be configured and the non-linear configuration mode, which allows you to jump around in the process at will, thus making it easier to adjust a setting

---

you made earlier without undoing all the changes in between. The drawback to all of this is a more confusing install routine that may cause new Linux users to accidentally skip a configuration setting or two. That said, as an experienced Linux user, I find YaST the most useful of the GUI installers. It also provides the ability to resize Windows NTFS partitions, which makes it a good choice of distribution if you want to dual-boot with Windows.

Configuration

YaST continues to be the tool of choice for configuration of your SUSE system. Like the Mandrake Control Center, YaST is a central configuration panel for most of the tools you'll need to set up your system. Like the installer, you'll find this control center both powerful and a little daunting. My suggestion is that you click through everything early on to figure out which control applet contains which type of settings. Later, when you actually have a problem, you should have a good idea where to go for the fix. A second control center devoted to X configuration is called SaX. My two complaints about YaST as a configuration tool are that it takes too long to load and that some of the tools will overwrite changes in a configuration file you've made by hand.

Package Management

Try to guess the name of the tool SUSE uses to add, remove, and upgrade programs. If you said YaST, you're right. This do-it-all tool also handles package management chores for SUSE. It truly is a one-stop experience. SUSE is an RPM-based distribution, like Fedora and Mandrake, and suffers from the limitations of that package format. In my experience, though, it has done a better job of overcoming dependency problems, particularly when the time comes to remove a program.

Documentation

The boxed set of SUSE comes with two books: a users' guide and a system administration guide. These books are also available in the online help system. However, documentation is not so plentiful on the Internet—at least not in English. A good place to start is *http://www.suseroot.com*. Besides being a valuable site in its own right, it has a page that links you to other helpful web sites. The URL is *http://www.suseroot.com/suse-linux-help.php*. Like Mandrake, I consider SUSE a good distribution for beginning Linux users. Like Gentoo, I also consider it a great distribution for more advanced users, programmers, and system administrators.

OpenSUSE

During LinuxWorld San Francisco in 2005, Novell announced that they were opening the development of SUSE Linux in a manner similar to what Red Hat did with Fedora. The main web site for this project is at *http://www.opensuse.org*.

I'm excited about this development. I believe it will lead to increased community involvement, improved community-developed documentation, and an increased user base, because the distribution will be freely available using convenient access methods (no need to perform FTP installs). I'm also hopeful that the community will adopt a command-line package management tool.

Ubuntu

Ubuntu is a new distribution that is based upon the venerable Debian. As this is a desktop pocket guide, I will focus upon Ubuntu because it has increasingly become the de facto Debian desktop distribution. The main web site for Ubuntu is *http://www.ubuntulinux.org*. Ubuntu receives corporate backing from Canonical Ltd., but it remains entirely free in all uses of the word. Pronunciation is usually *oo-BOON-too*.

The Ubuntu project made a big splash with its first release in late 2004. Not only was it eagerly embraced by Debian users tired of waiting for the long-delayed release of Debian 3.1, it also picked up distro switchers who were happy to find an easy-to-install and -maintain desktop-oriented version of Linux. To top it all off, Canonical offered to ship free CDs to anyone who requested and ended up shipping more than a million. Within months, this distribution had risen from obscurity to sitting at the top of the Distrowatch rankings (*http://www.distrowatch.com*).

Ubuntu comes in two forms: a live CD and an install CD. Both can be freely downloaded from the Ubuntu web site and are available as torrents. The live CD is rather interesting—not only will it let you run Ubuntu on the fly from the CD, but it also includes Windows installers for a few cross-platform open source applications like OpenOffice.org and Firefox. Just stick the CD in the drive while using Windows to access these programs. You can obtain either CD from the Ubuntu web site. A new version of Ubuntu is planned every six months, but you don't need to install from the CD each time. The package management program, described shortly, allows you to update your current install to all of the latest package versions with just a simple command or two.

The default Ubuntu desktop is a very up-to-date GNOME. If you prefer KDE, you are free to install it later; if you prefer a completely GNOME-free desktop, install the Ubuntu derivative Kubuntu. It's the same distro with a different default desktop.

Ubuntu does not install any non-free (as in free licensed) software by default, which means that its multimedia support is rather weak until you add additional software—you can't even play MP3 files. However, adding the required support is quite simple, as documented on the Ubuntu Wiki; some tips are provided in Chapter 6.

Installation

Installation of Ubuntu is fairly simple, if a little on the drab side—Ubuntu comes with a text-based installer only. Still, it has all the tools you need to set up Ubuntu quickly. The downside is that you can't customize the packages you want installed (beyond a single minimal install choice). This isn't so bad because the default install has pretty much the programs everyone wants to install on their machine anyway. Of course, having more flexibility would be better. Although you can't resize existing Windows partitions, you can still set up a dual-boot system if there is free space available.

Configuration

The install routine does a fairly good job of setting up most of your hardware, leaving little for you to configure afterwards. However, you still have to take extra steps to configure most wireless network cards, 3D graphic acceleration for NVIDIA and ATI cards, and printers. In addition, Ubuntu doesn't include anything that isn't free, so you'll have to manually install packages like Java and MP3 support. Configuring devices and adding non-free software involves using a mix of standalone GUI tools and editing configuration files—nothing difficult, but some of it is not intuitive if you are not familiar with Debian-derived distributions. The online documentation at the main web site comes in handy here.

Package Management

Package management is the same as with its Debian parent—which means it's fantastic. Ubuntu uses the *apt* system to figure out program dependencies and download all the needed packages for you automatically. The installer is very easy to use on the command line, as is the included graphical installer Synaptic. If you've never experienced the wonderfulness of the apt package manager, you should give Ubuntu a try for this reason alone.

My only gripe is the difficulty in installing very large programs that are made up of a lot of components, such as KDE. Most distributions provide a meta-package called KDE that installs all the necessary software, but Ubuntu (and Debian) require you to select all the components yourself. Don't get me wrong—it still handles dependencies—it just doesn't roll everything up in one easy selection. This makes it flexible, because you don't need to install unwanted software, but also annoying, because there are dozens of KDE options, which makes it difficult to know which ones you should select to give you the software you desire.

Documentation

Despite its youth, Ubuntu already has terrific community-created documentation in the form of a Wiki (*http://wiki.ubuntu.com*) and a forum (*http://ubuntuforums.org*). I've found the Wiki to be the best stopping place to learn how to install Java or get 3D video acceleration working, and the forum is the best place to search for troubleshooting help.

The combination of good default configuration; easy-to-use package management; quality documentation; and a large, active user community makes Ubuntu a superb option for your desktop distribution for beginners and advanced users alike.

Other Distributions

The main tracking web site for Linux distributions is *http://www.distrowatch.com*. Here you will find news and information of practically every public distribution in existence—there are more than 300! A column on the right ranks the distributions based upon the number of clicks each distribution gets on this web site. Though this ranking would seem to be a perfect indicator of popularity, it is misleading. For one thing, it indicates which distributions are currently getting the most attention, not which ones have the most users.

Also, users can vote for each distribution multiple times, which means that some distributions might have artificially inflated numbers.

Here are brief descriptions of a few other distributions worth looking at sometime:

Knoppix

Using Knoppix, you can run Linux completely from a CD without having to install anything to your hard drive. This distro is a great way to try out Linux without committing a lot of time or effort to the endeavor. Knoppix does a great job of detecting and setting up your computer hardware, and many people use it as a quick test to find out whether a computer they are about to purchase will work well with Linux. Visit *http://www.knoppix.net* for more information. O'Reilly offers documentation on Knoppix in the form of *Knoppix Hacks* and the *Knoppix Pocket Reference*.

Linspire

This is a purely desktop-oriented distribution that focuses upon ease of use and attempts to be as Windows-like as possible. If all you want out of your Linux experience is a secure and stable replacement for Windows, try this distribution. Besides an easy install, Linspire provides an easy-to-use package management program with their CNR (click 'n' run) service. With just a couple of mouse clicks, you can install hundreds of programs. Unfortunately, this service will cost you about $50 a year to use. Linspire supports only KDE, however, so if you prefer GNOME or another desktop environment, it isn't for you. For more information, visit *http://www.linspire.com*.

Slackware

Slackware is the oldest Linux distribution that has been in continual development. Mostly a one-man show, this distribution is often regarded as being the most "Unix-like" of the Linux distributions, which basically means that it lets you configure everything yourself and doesn't hold your hand while you do it. This isn't to say it is difficult to set up, just that it has a clean, simple method of configuration that won't do anything unexpected, like launch a GUI tool to overwrite the X configuration file you just spent the last 20 minutes tweaking. Slackware has a lot of "mature" users and often attracts new users who are tired of the complexity of other distributions. The web site is *http://www.slackware.org*.

Xandros

The folks at Xandros have done a great job of producing a Linux replacement for Windows, particularly for business users. Out of the box, Xandros can authenticate users against a Windows directory server and can browse Windows network shares. In addition, some versions of Xandros come with Codeweavers CrossOver Office, which lets you install the Windows version of several important programs such as Microsoft Office, Quicken, and Photoshop. Xandros is a Debian-based distribution, and it has the same ease of use with regard to program installation as Ubuntu, but its default has you install software from Xandros Networks. Personally, I find Xandros a little too Windows-like for my tastes, but new Linux users may find it the best way to make the transition. For more information, visit *http://www.xandros.com*. *Linux Made Easy* (No Starch Press) is an excellent book on Xandros.

Getting a Distribution

The retail software market is dominated by Microsoft and Windows software. It's not even easy to find stores that carry Macintosh software, and finding Linux is yet more difficult. Here are the various channels you can use to obtain a Linux distribution:

Retail stores

Most Linux distributions have stopped selling in the retail channel. I imagine this is because frequent updates to the software, coupled with low sales volume, lead to a lot of returns. At this time, you have a reasonable chance of finding SUSE and Linspire in CompUSA, and SUSE in Best Buy and Fry's. In other words, your choice is extremely limited.

Online stores

Major brick-and-mortar retailers seldom carry more online than they do in their stores, so you're more likely to find Linux sold online by second-tier vendors. Amazon is a notable exception. Each distribution provider is likely to sell products direct from their web site or allow you to download the software for free. Optionally, you can visit *http://www.cheapbytes.com* or *http://www.lincd.com*, where you can purchase cheap, legal copies of a distribution. Of course, this version doesn't include support from the original vendor.

Free downloads

Many Linux distributions are available at no cost. Projects such as Fedora, Gentoo, and Ubuntu make the complete distribution available for free at their respective web sites. Ubuntu will even mail you a free CD. Mandriva makes community editions that have a slightly smaller feature set and no support available for free download. Linux CDs and DVDs are usually made available as an ISO file. These files, which are often around 650 MB in size, represent a complete CD image and can be burned to CD with any burning software. There are also numerous web sites where you can find ISOs of various distributions available for free download—most of these are BitTorrent sites. A particularly useful site is *http://www.linuxisotorrent.com*.

## CHAPTER 2

Logging In

It probably seems silly to devote a whole chapter to logging in. After all, what is there to it besides typing in a username and password? Quite a lot, actually, but none of it is particularly difficult. I just don't want you to get hung up at the login screen and not know exactly what to do.

Graphical Logins

Most distributions boot to a graphical login manager. When you type in your username and password, you are logged in to the default desktop environment. If this isn't the desktop you want, you'll need to configure the login manager to load an alternate desktop. This is pretty simple to do.

The login manager for Fedora and Ubuntu is called the GNOME Display Manager (GDM). It's configured to log you in to GNOME automatically. To log in to a different installed desktop environment, look for the icon on the login screen labeled Session Type or something similar. Click it, make a selection, then log in. GDM requires you to press Enter (or Return) between typing your username and password.

An alternative way to perform this switch in Fedora is to run the program *switchdesk*. If you are in X, it launches a GUI program that lets you select the default desktop for the current user. If you run it at the command line, you must specify a desktop environment to switch to, like this:

```
$ switchdesk kde
```

The only other option is gnome.

The login manager for Mandriva and SUSE is called the KDE Display Manager (KDM). To change your default desktop, click Menu → Session Type, make a selection, then log in. Each display manager remembers your desktop choice on a per-user basis.

As a Gentoo user, your display manager is whichever one you configured it to be when you modified your *letc/rc.conf* file during system configuration. In case you skipped that step when you set up Gentoo, use your favorite text editor to modify the following line of *letc/rc.conf*:

```
DISPLAYMANAGER="xdm"
```

Simply change xdm to gdm or kdm. Next, tell Gentoo to load the display manager when it starts up by adding the */etc/init.d/ xdm* init script to your default runlevel. Here is the command for this step:

```
$ sudo rc-update add xdm default
```

Confusingly, the init script is always *xdm*, even when you are running a different display manager.

Text Logins

Some people have their system set to boot to text mode, then they log in, and finally launch a desktop environment if they so choose. This setup is less common than it once was, but some people find that they like the flexibility this method provides. If you want to give it a try, there are a couple of things you need to configure.

First, you need to make sure that your system boots to text mode, which is usually done by controlling the runlevel the system boots to. The following list explains how you control it for each distribution:

Fedora, Mandriva, and SUSE

In your */etc/inittab* file, modify the line that reads id:5: initdefault: to read id:**3**:initdefault:.

Gentoo

By default, Gentoo boots in text mode. If you have already configured it otherwise, the easiest solution is to remove *xdm* from your default startup scripts. Use this command to do this: **rc-update del xdm default**.

Ubuntu

Similar to Gentoo, to prevent booting to X in Ubuntu, you must remove *gdm* from the startup scripts. To do this, use this command: **update-rc.d -f gdm remove**. If you ever want to change back, use this command: **update-rc.d gdm defaults**.

Now that you are booting to a console, your next question might be how to get into X and a desktop environment when you really want them. Table 2-1 lists the command-line names for various desktop environments and window managers; enter this name in a file in your home directory called *.xinitrc* (you'll need to create this file if it doesn't exist). Here is how this file looks if you want to start KDE when you launch X:

```
startkde
```

That's it. Now, when you want to run X, just enter **startx** at the console prompt; it reads the value you placed in *.xinitrc* and loads the appropriate environment.

Table 2-1. Desktop environment and window manager command-line names

Desktop environment	Command-line name
GNOME	gnome-session
KDE	startkde
Blackbox	blackbox

Table 2-1. Desktop environment and window manager command-line names (continued)

Desktop environment	Command-line name
Enlightenment	enlightenment
Fluxbox	startfluxbox
IceWM	icewm
XFce 4	startxvfce4
WindowMaker	wmaker

TIP

You can actually put more information in your *.xinitrc* file if you want other programs to load as well. For example:

```
konsole -geometry 600x900+27+300 &
mozilla-firefox &
startkde
```

This time, when X and KDE load, you'll have the virtual terminal Konsole running with a specific size and location, and the web browser Firefox will launch. The ampersand after the first two lines means to execute this command and continue on. You don't want to put that after the desktop environment start command, as it will launch and then exit immediately, taking you back to the command line.

## CHAPTER 3

GNOME

GNOME is one of the two most popular desktop environments for Linux, and it is the default GUI for the Fedora and Ubuntu distributions. Gentoo does not favor a particular desktop environment and provides pretty much the same GNOME experience as you would get by installing GNOME manually.

Because it is impossible in a book this size to describe every minor difference between each distribution's GNOME implementation, I'll have to shoot for the largest target, Fedora, and hope that the information I give can be used with only minor adjustments with any other configuration of GNOME. Usually the only differences are placement of menu choices and subtle variations in menu and option names.

GNOME Desktop

Once you log in to GNOME, you'll find that it resembles a Macintosh layout more than Windows. This is because most GNOME setups place a panel along the top and bottom of the screen. The panel at the top commonly holds one or more menus, several quick-launch icons, and, at the far right, the clock, applets, and notifications are displayed. The panel on the bottom acts as a taskbar and displays a desktop pager to allow you to switch between virtual desktops (commonly called *workspaces*).

The basic use of the desktop environment is as you'd expect. Click once on menu and panel icons, double-click desktop icons to launch the programs, and right-click anywhere you're curious to see if there are options available on a context-sensitive menu.

You can freely move items in the panels (even to other panels), add new items, and delete existing ones. To do this, either right-click on an item to move or delete it, or right-click an empty space to add new items. All of the applets that you can add to the panel are conveniently located in a single-level menu with basic descriptions of each choice. Each panel also has its own properties, which you can access from the right-click menu. In all, you'll find panel configuration and placement very flexible with GNOME, but with fewer options than what KDE gives you. This is one reason many people like GNOME—simplicity.

This simplicity extends to other areas. For example, most configuration dialogs don't require you to click OK or Apply for your changes to take affect. Instead, they happen instantly. This is slightly disconcerting at first, especially when making changes to options on a tab—you might worry that switching to another tab will cause you to lose your settings. Don't worry, the changes are always saved.

Most distributions place launchers for programs and utilities into special-purpose menus placed on the left side of the top panel. Having more than one high-level menu leads to less clutter in the menus themselves and makes it easier for you to find what you want. In Fedora Core 4, these menus are:

Applications
> This is the typical program launcher menu you expect to find on a panel.

Places

The links here open specific places on your filesystem. The Computer link displays your storage devices, while "Connect to Server" option opens a dialog where you can connect to a remote server using a limited set of protocols.

Desktop

You can log off or lock your screen from here. More importantly, you can configure your desktop under the Preferences and System Settings menus. Preferences apply to your personal desktop, while System Settings allows you to make changes that affect the entire system for all users.

There are a few keyboard shortcuts, listed in Table 3-1, which you might find useful. You can modify these shortcuts, or create new ones, with the keyboard shortcut utility found at Desktop → Preferences → Keyboard Shortcuts.

Table 3-1. GNOME keyboard shortcuts

Keyboard shortcut	Action
Ctrl-Alt-right arrow	Moves to a desktop to the right of the current one.
Ctrl-Alt-left arrow	Moves to a desktop to the left of the current one.
Ctrl-Alt-up arrow	Moves you to one above your current desktop if there are multiple rows of desktops in the pager.
Ctrl-Alt-down arrow	Moves you to the desktop below your current one if there are multiple rows of desktops in the pager.
Shift-Ctrl-Alt-any arrow	Moves the active window to the workspace that sits in the direction of the arrow you click. This also makes the indicated workspace active.
Alt-Tab	Cycles through windows on the current desktop.
Alt-Shift-Tab	Cycles backward through the windows of the current desktop.
Ctrl-Alt-D	Toggles between minimizing and restoring all windows on the desktop.

Virtual Desktops and Window Management

GNOME supports the X feature known as virtual desktops. If you're not familiar with this feature, it may help to think of desktops like channels on a television set. You can view multiple channels on a TV, but only one at a time (I'm not including those of you with picture-in-a-picture sets). Virtual desktops work the same way: your computer can have multiple workspaces, each with its own set of windows, but you can view them only one at a time. Most distributions configure GNOME to display two or four virtual desktops, usually numbered 1 through 4.

You can use virtual desktops to relieve your display of some of the window clutter that inevitably happens when you are running multiple applications. Though you can randomly place windows all over your desktops, you may find it more helpful to group them by task, such as running email programs on Desktop 1, web browsers on 2, terminal sessions on 3, and image editing on 4. When you want to switch tasks, you can just switch desktops, which also helps your mind make a context switch from one task to another. You can configure GNOME to have as many as 36 workspaces (desktops), but having so many will probably cause more organizational problems than they solve.

Switching between virtual desktops is easy and user configurable. One way to switch desktops is to click the desktop pager in the lower-right corner of the screen. Each square represents a different desktop. Another is to use the keyboard shortcuts found in Table 3-1.

You can configure virtual desktops by right-clicking on the desktop pager and choosing Preferences. Your options here are to stack your desktops vertically as well as horizontally (which then allows you to use the up and down arrow shortcuts when switching desktops), add more workspaces, or name the workspaces.

With the ability to place windows on various workspaces comes the need for better ways to manage your windows. For example, when you click on a web link in an email, it will open a web browser on your current desktop. But because you do all of your browsing on another desktop and you want to keep this window open for awhile, you need to be able to move it to where it belongs.

Doing this is quite simple. You can right-click on the titlebar for the web browser, choose "Move to Another Workspace," and select the appropriate one. Or, you can use the keyboard shortcut to move a window, which is simply a variation on the "switch workspace" commands in Table 3-1 that requires you to use the Shift modifier. For example, to move a window to a desktop to the right, press Shift-Ctrl-Alt-right arrow. This trick has the added convenience of moving the window and switching focus to the indicated desktop automatically.

GNOME also allows you to set a window to appear on all desktops by using the option "Always on Visible Workspace" from the titlebar's right-click menu. You can also set a window to always be on top of others from the same menu. This feature is handy when you have an application you want to "float" above all the other windows, like a control window for a CD or music player.

A few more window management features are available by selecting Desktop → Preferences → Window Preferences. These include the ability to make a window active just by moving your mouse over it (this is called "focus follows mouse" and takes a bit of getting used to) and the ability to control what happens when you double-click a window's titlebar. The Movement Key option allows you to specify which key must be held down to be able to click and drag a window to a new location. Remembering this key is very useful, as it allows you to grab the window anywhere, not just on the titlebar.

Fast User Switching and Sessions

Linux is a multiuser operating system, which means that it is capable of having more than one user running applications on it at once. This concept is easy to understand when you are running in a server environment and everyone is accessing the machine remotely, but it's a little more difficult when you only have one keyboard, mouse, and monitor. In fact, Linux's multiuser nature would almost seem useless in this case. But that isn't true. Think of all the times you've been working and your child or spouse wanted to use the machine for a few minutes. You're happy to let them do so, but you don't want them to make changes to your settings or what you are currently working on. You also don't want to close your programs and log off. To solve this problem, you can make use of GNOME's Fast User Switching ability, which leaves your programs running, but starts a new session just for your guest user.

To do this, click Applications → System Tools → New Login, which will instantly lock your current session (so prying eyes can't get in without your password), and switch you to a new login screen. Once your guest user logs in, he has complete access to his account and desktop settings, just as if you were not using the computer at all. To switch back to your session, repeat the process, but this time, when you run New Login, you'll be greeted with a dialog that lets you either create another new session or switch to an existing one. If you switch, you may have to hit a key to see the password prompt to disable the screensaver. The same thing happens when you log off the guest login.

The multiple logins each run on their own virtual terminal (not to be confused with a virtual desktop). Your system is usually configured with about 12 of these. Terminals 1 through 6 are text-only, and 7 through 12 are graphical. To switch between them, use the shortcut Ctrl-Alt-F1...F12.

Throughout my description of Fast User Switching, I used the word "session." A session is merely the state of your current login. It denotes which programs you are running, where they are located, the size of the windows, and any other status information. A session can be saved and revisited each time you log in to your computer.

Setting this up is not difficult. Configure your session the way you want it, complete with applications you want to run each time you log in, placed exactly where you want them to appear. Then click Desktop → Log Out, and, in the dialog that appears, check the box for "Save current setup" and finish logging out. This step saves your session as the new default and restores everything the next time you log in. Well, maybe not everything. The Firefox web browser, for example, cannot be saved in a session, but there is a way to work around this limitation using the session preference panel found at Desktop → Preferences → More Preferences → Sessions. On the last tab, Startup Programs, you can click Add to tell the session manager to load specified programs automatically on startup.

I have to admit that, using both Fedora and Ubuntu, I have not been able to save more than one session, the default. The problem is that when I log on, I am not given the choice of which session to start—the default session always runs. Still, being able to save even just one configuration can be very useful.

File Manager

GNOME includes the excellent file manager Nautilus, which was originally developed as a standalone program (not intended for any particular desktop) by the company Eazel. Eazel eventually closed its doors and the code was adopted by the GNOME project to become their featured file manager.

To open Nautilus, double-click your home icon on the desktop. You're presented with a small window displaying the contents of your home directory, which at this point may contain just the single directory *Desktop*. Double-click this to open it. This action opens another window almost directly over your current one. Move this window to the side, resize it by grabbing an edge and dragging, and then close it. Now, open it again. It will open at the new location and size you just set it at.

Nautilus's default setting of opening each directory in a new window, and remembering the size and location of that window, is known as spatial view. This controversial way of viewing your filesystem is actually quite old—Windows 95 and the classic Mac OS worked this way. Some people love it because it encourages them to create flat directory structures, and they come to think of the location of a directory or file in the filesystem as being the same as its physical location on the screen.

Others abhor spatial view, and if you are one of them, you probably want to know how to turn it off. Go to Desktop → Preferences → File Management. Under the Behavior tab, check "Always open in browser windows." Another way to get to this choice—from any Nautilus window—is to click Edit → Preferences. Now, close any Nautilus windows you have open and then reopen one. You'll see that Nautilus has added a toolbar (reminiscent of a web browser) and a sidebar. (I'm going to assume you've turned off spatial view for the rest of my coverage of Nautilus.)

The Nautilus Preferences menu deserves a little bit more attention. Using it, you can specify whether folders are displayed in list view as icons, control the size of the list or icons, choose what information displays under each icon, control the columns that display in list view, and specify what types of files are previewed. There aren't a lot of settings here, but they are conveniently grouped in one place and are easy to understand.

In basic use, Nautilus works just like any other file manager. You drag and drop files to move them, or use the shortcuts Ctrl-C, Ctrl-X, and Ctrl-V to copy, cut, and paste, respectively. The default action of dragging a file to a new location is to move it. You can modify this with a couple of keyboard shortcuts. Hold the Ctrl key while dragging to create a copy in the new location, or hold Ctrl-Shift while dragging to create a link to the file in the new location. A link is simply a pointer to the original file. A double-click on a link to a folder opens the folder, and a link to a document opens the document. Links are convenient ways to access files from different locations without copying the files all over the place and ending up with different versions.

Nautilus has a few really cool features. From any Nautilus window, click Edit → Backgrounds and Emblems. This opens a window with three icons on the left that control the choices available on the right. Using this window, you can drag and drop patterns, colors, and emblems onto files, folders, the information pane, and the file viewing pane. Using these decorations, you can easily create an interesting look for your file manager, as well as distinguish important files from one another.

You'll also notice that the sidebar on the left has a drop-down list. What you select here controls what is displayed in the sidebar. One of the selections is Notes, which lets you type in information about the contents of the active folder. Once you do this, a note emblem is added to the folder icon, and thereafter you can view the notes by clicking the small yellow note icon at the top of the sidebar. These notes are a convenient way to remind yourself exactly what is in a folder.

Nautilus includes the ability to burn a CD. This is an interesting feature that makes it very convenient to create data backups. To use this feature, open Nautilus and click Go → CD Creator. This takes you to the *burn:///* folder. Copy the files you want to burn to the CD here, insert a blank CD, and then click "Write contents to CD." This step opens a simple dialog where you can tweak a few things before actually burning the CD.

Finally, you can use Nautilus to connect to remote file-systems. GNOME supports just a few remote protocols, but it includes some big ones: SMB (Server Message Block) for connecting to Windows machines, SFTP (Secure File Transfer Protocol) for connecting to Linux machines, and FTP (File Transfer Protocol) for connecting to FTP sites to retrieve software. There are two ways to use this feature. You can type the protocol handlers from Table 3-2 and the remote machine name directly into the Location field of Nautilus (View → Address bar), or you can select Places → Connect to Server and fill out the dialog box that appears. The advantage of the second method is that it creates an icon on your desktop that you can use to connect in the future. Right-click and choose Unmount to remove this icon.

Table 3-2. Protocol handlers for Nautilus

Protocol handler	Use to
smb:///	Connect to remote Windows shares.
sftp:///	Connect to any remote system with a running SSH daemon.
dav:///	Connect to a WebDAV server.
davs:///	Connect to a secure WebDAV server.
ftp:///	Connect to an FTP server.

The GNOME Menu and Program Launchers

When you install a new program, it may or may not add an icon to launch the program in the GNOME Applications menu. If it does, great; if it doesn't, you have a little bit of work to do to make it convenient to launch the program without using the command line or a Run dialog.

Prior to Version 2.8, GNOME came with a simple menu editor that you could access from Nautilus using the protocol handler application:///. In version 2.10, GNOME dropped support for this, but no menu editor was ready to take its place. Starting with Version 2.12 (not yet released), a new menu editor, *gmenu-simple-editor*, exists, but it currently allows you to hide and unhide menu entries only, not create new ones.

Obviously, work is in progress to improve the menu-editing situation, but what are you to do until it is complete? Well, an independent programmer has created a utility called the Simple Menu Editor for GNOME, or *smeg* for short. It is in the Universe repository in Ubuntu, and the FedoraFAQ (*http://www.fedorafaq.org*) points to *http://foolish.digitalinc. info/pakker/i386/* as a place to get RPMs. Once installed, you can use this utility to add new folders to the Applications menu, hide or delete existing folders, add your own custom launchers, or delete existing ones. The program is a work in progress, so check for updates frequently.

You can also create an icon on your desktop that can launch a program. Just right-click on the desktop and choose Create Launcher. Fill out the information fields in the dialog that appears. The only two that are required are a name and the command to launch the program. If you click the box labeled Icon, you can select an icon image. Click OK when done and you'll have a new program launcher on your desktop.

GNOME Configuration

Almost all the configuration worth doing on a GNOME system can be handled by the applets found under the Desktop → Preferences, and Desktop → System Settings menus. As I mentioned earlier, the first group of programs affect the settings for the currently logged in user and the second group are system-wide settings that affect all users. You'll need to know the root password to run those programs. SUSE replaces Preferences with a GNOME Control Center and replaces System Settings with YaST.

I've already introduced the Session, File Management, keyboard shortcuts, and Windows preference panels. Several others have very obvious uses, like Desktop Background and Screensaver. Here are descriptions of a few of the more interesting or useful ones:

Font

> Besides the obvious use of choosing the system-wide fonts, this utility also lets you set anti-aliasing. Here's where the real-time changes of GNOME come in handy. With a page of text open in the background, click on each option in the "Font Rendering and Details" sections and watch the changes on the background text. This feature makes it very easy to pick the settings you like best.

Keyboard

> Here you can select which keyboard model you have (which includes many models that have extra multimedia keys), as well as specify the keyboard layout for your language. There are also several excellent options under Layout Options that you should explore to see whether any meet your particular needs. The settings on the last tab (Typing Break) let you set a time interval to lock your screen, in order to force you to take a break from typing.

Remote Desktop

> When you enable desktop sharing through this applet, other people will be able to connect to your desktop using VNC.

Removable Drives and Media

> The settings in this panel determine what happens when you insert various types of removable media, such as audio and blank CDs, DVDs, and USB storage devices.

Screen Resolution

With this applet, you can set your screen resolution when you log into GNOME. This setting does not apply to other users or to the login screen. The values here are determined by those entered in your *xorg.conf* file, which I cover in Chapter 7.

Theme

The visual appearance of the GNOME windows is controlled by the theme you choose in this configuration screen. This is another place where GNOME's instant changes are useful, as you can see the results of you selection in near real time.

More Preferences → Preferred Applications

Use this applet to specify which program should be opened when you click on web addresses, mailto links, and when opening a terminal.

The configuration programs under the System Settings menu affect all users and are often specific to a particular distribution. The ones I describe here are in Fedora Core 4 and Ubuntu and may not be in your particular version of GNOME.

Server Settings → Services (Fedora)

Use this program to specify which services should load when your computer boots. For example, if you've installed Samba and you're told to run the daemon when your computer boots, this is where you set it (if you don't know how to do it from the command line).

Add/Remove Applications (Fedora)

This program would seem to be the answer to your program installation dreams—but it's not. This is a simple utility that lets you add and remove the programs available on the Fedora CD. It is of no use for installing other programs or newer versions of programs on the CD.

Synaptic Package Manager (Ubuntu)

This is a GUI frontend for the apt system, and it allows you to add, remove, and update your programs.

Date & Time

Sets the system date and time. Also of interest is the Network Time Protocol tab, where you can request that your system time be updated against time servers on the Internet, thus always keeping your clock accurate.

Display (Fedora)

Yet another place to configure your screen resolution, as well as your color depth, monitor type, and video card. The Dual head tab lets you easily set up a monitor in conjunction with your laptop, or two monitors with a desktop machine.

Login Screen

Here you can set up how the GNOME login screen (GDM) appears.

Network

Fedora and Ubuntu both have networking applets, but the actual programs differ. Basically, you can use this applet to control the network interfaces that Linux is aware of. As outlined in Chapter 6, sometimes configuration from the command line is necessary before the interface is even visible in this program.

Printer

Lets you set up new printers for your computer. The default print system is CUPS, and if you have a CUPS server on your network, configuration is automatic.

Users and Groups

A nice graphical way to manage your users and groups.

If you're interested in creating a highly customized appearance for your GNOME desktop, check out all the wallpapers, themes, and icons available at *http://www.gnome-look.org*.

## CHAPTER 4

KDE

KDE is another popular desktop environment for Linux, and it is the default GUI for Mandriva and SUSE. Gentoo does not favor a particular desktop environment and provides much the same KDE experience as you would get by installing KDE manually. If you're interested in the Ubuntu distribution, but prefer KDE, then you might consider installing Kubuntu, which is just like Ubuntu, except that it installs KDE instead of GNOME. You can also install KDE on Fedora, but what you'll get is an oddly themed version that feels very GNOME-like. You may not enjoy it.

KDE is highly configurable—perhaps too much so. Many of the complaints you'll find about it concern how cluttered the toolbars and menus are or how many options are in each configuration window. However, you can make use of these features and create a very customized desktop environment that works the way you want it to. There is some talk about limiting the extreme configurability of KDE in upcoming releases, possibly as early as Version 4.0, which will be out in late 2006.

As I did with GNOME, I'm not going to describe exactly how KDE looks or operates on each distribution. Instead, I'll describe a generic install of KDE, and that information will be 98 percent applicable to the distribution you use. Any variation from your distribution should be small enough that you can easily overcome it by looking under a different menu or looking for option labels that are similar to the ones I mention here.

The KDE Desktop

Once you log into KDE, you are presented with a desktop pretty similar to Windows XP. The display is filled with a background image, icons, and a panel running along the bottom of the screen. All of these things will work pretty much as you'd expect. However, there are some features that are not immediately obvious or that have more functions than their Windows counterparts, and those are what I'll talk about.

First off is the *kicker*, which is the panel along the bottom of the screen. This panel contains the usual culprits: a program menu called the K Menu in the lower-left corner (usually represented by a big K, a gear icon, a distribution logo icon, or the word Start); icons to launch popular programs with a single click; a taskbar area that can display icons of your running programs; and a system tray area that contains applets like a lock screen tool, virtual desktop pager, and a clock. The panel can be moved to different edges by clicking on a blank area of the panel and dragging it to the new edge. Right-click on the menu icon and expand the Panel Menu option to reveal several options for adding programs to the panel or customizing its use. Here are some descriptions of the major categories:

Panel Menu → Configure Panel

> This option opens a configuration window with dozens of options for configuring the kicker panel. Here you'll find options to change the location of the panel, its size,

how to hide it, and how the taskbar behaves. You can have more than one panel, and the options you select here affect whichever panel you've selected in the "Settings for" drop-down list.

Panel Menu → Add to Panel → Applet

Applets are small applications that are embedded in the panel to add extra functionality. KDE comes with a couple dozen, but these are the ones I've found most useful (excluding the defaults of clock and pager):

Dictionary

This is an embedded version of the standalone program *kdict* that places a small field on your taskbar. Type a word in this field and press Enter to execute a search of several online dictionaries.

Klipper

This applet stores multiple levels of "clippings" so you can paste them into new documents or data fields. Click the panel icon to select the clipping to paste. You can use the standard keyboard shortcuts of Ctrl-C to Copy, Ctrl-X to Cut, and Ctrl-V to Paste. In addition, you can copy text in Linux (X, actually) by highlighting the text, positioning your cursor where you want to copy it to, and clicking your middle-mouse button (or the scroll wheel if you have that, or both mouse buttons if you have only two). There's no need to use a keyboard at all!

Storage Media

When you select this applet, nothing appears to happen to your panel. However, once you attach an external storage device or insert a music CD, an icon appears. Click on this icon to reveal several choices for accessing the device. Click again before removing the device to choose the option Safely Remove, then remove the device a few seconds later.

Panel Menu → Add to Panel → Application

Use this option to navigate the menu of applications and select a launcher to add to the panel. You can also add items to the panel by opening the K Menu, navigating to the launcher, right-clicking upon it, and choosing "Add item to Main Panel." You can even add an entire submenu this way.

Panel Menu → Add to Panel → Panel

KDE has several types of panels, all of which are listed here. The external taskbar shows your running program icons in a separate strip from the kicker, which is particularly useful when you mount the kicker on the side of the screen (you should remember to remove the embedded taskbar by choosing Panel Menu → Remove From Panel → Applet → Taskbar). An alternative taskbar called the KasBar displays large preview images of your running applications, making it easier to choose from among them.

Panel Menu → Add to Panel → Special Button

Select any of these options to add a special purpose button to the panel. I've found the Quickbrowser and the Konqueror Profiles buttons most useful. The first lets you access a specific directory with a single click, and the second launches Konqueror (file manager and web browser) with specific settings. You have to configure the Konqueror profile first, and I show you how to do that in the section "File Manager," later in this chapter.

Most items that you add to the panel have special properties that you can access by left- or right-clicking on its icon. To remove an item from the panel, look for a Remove option when you click on its icon. Some items can be removed only if you click on the small "handle" that sits beside the applet, or if you select it from the Panel Menu → Remove From Panel menu.

Virtual Desktops and Window Management

KDE offers more than a dozen ways to manipulate application windows. Learning these methods can enhance your productivity and create an uncluttered desktop. In addition to these window management features, KDE makes good use of X's virtual desktop ability.

If you aren't familiar with virtual desktops, it may help to think of them as being like different channels on a television. Dozens of channels are being sent to your television, but you only view one at a time. Likewise, you can have several virtual desktops, each displaying different windows, but you only view one desktop at a time.

Most distributions come configured to support two or four virtual desktops, usually numbered 1 through 4. You can place the windows of running applications on specific desktops and switch to them as needed. This approach means that open windows are not in your way when they are on different desktops, which helps keep your desktop environment clean and tidy and makes you more productive. Many people place specific types of applications on each desktop. For example, web browsers on desktop 1, email on 2, terminal sessions on 3, and text editors on 4. Switching between desktops is very easy. You can use the pager embedded in the panel—just click on a number to make the switch—but better still is to use the keyboard shortcuts listed in Table 4-1. These shortcuts, like many others, can be configured in the KDE Control Center with the Regional & Accessibility → Keyboard Shortcuts applet.

Table 4-1. Virtual desktop keyboard shortcuts

Keyboard shortcut	Action
Ctrl-Tab	Cycles virtual desktops in ascending order.
Ctrl-Shift-Tab	Cycles virtual desktops in descending order.
Ctrl-F1, F2, F3, etc.	Switches to a specific desktop numbered 1–12.
Ctrl-Shift-F1, F2, F3, etc.	Switches to a specific desktop numbered 13–20.

An application window is associated with the desktop you opened it on. You can easily move the window to a different desktop afterwards by right-clicking on the titlebar, choosing To Desktop, and selecting a desktop to send the window to.

You'll notice that the To Desktop menu has an option to have a window appear on All Desktops. This is handy when you have a program you want easy access to at all times, like a chat window or media player. To make this even more useful, some people enable the option from the titlebar's right-click menu, Advanced → Keep Above Others, which causes the window to float, even above the active application window, the way a lot of toolbars and palettes work in programs like Photoshop or the GIMP.

An application can be forced to appear on specific desktops and with specific dimensions when you open it. To do this, open the application, right-click the titlebar, then select Advanced → Specific Window Settings. A dialog will open with several tabs and a lot of options. The focus is on the Geometry tab; this tab and the Preferences tab have the options you'll most often set. Check the box of the option you want to enable and specify a value. The drop-down box has four options:

Do Not Affect
> Obviously, it means your settings won't have any effect. It's pretty much the same as disabling an option.

Apply Initially
> Apply your settings when the program is first launched, but you can change it later as desired. When you close the program, it will "forget" any changes.

Remember
> Apply your settings when the program is launched, allow you to change those settings later, and then remember those changes. For example, a program set to open on desktop 1 can be moved to desktop 2, closed, and when you launch it again, it will be on desktop 2, not 1.

Force

> Just as it says. This forces the window manager to use your defined settings, and it won't allow you to change these settings through normal means—say, moving a window from one desktop to another or resizing it by grabbing the edges.

The size of a window is specified as comma-separated width and height measurements expressed in pixels. For example, to set a window to 300 pixels wide by 100 pixels high, you would enter the value **300,100**. Likewise, the position of a window is expressed as XY coordinates starting from the top-left corner of the screen. These coordinates specify where the top-left corner of the window appears; then the size measurements take over. For example, to force a window to appear 20 pixels over from the left and 150 pixels down from the top, enter the value **20,150**.

WARNING

If you're familiar with positioning windows via coordinates, you may be tempted to use negative values to specify a position from the right or bottom edges, but it doesn't work, and instead places items completely offscreen. If this happens to you, press Alt-F3 to bring up the Window Properties dialog so you can make an adjustment.

There are more, and more advanced, window features than these to help you manage your running applications and desktop. You can access these features from the titlebar right-click option Configure Window Behavior, which opens a rather complex configuration dialog that allows you to set global window settings. Many of these settings are duplicated in the KDE Control Center, but I'll describe them here because they specifically have to do with window management. Here are brief descriptions of the various settings, grouped by the icon you use to access the settings:

Window Decorations

Here you can specify the decorations that appear around the edge of a window. Distributions come with different decorations, and a few have a distribution-specific decoration. Use your package management search tool to look for more KDE decorations or visit *http://www.kde-look.org*. You can also choose which buttons (minimize, maximize, close, help) appear on your titlebar and their location.

Actions

Here you can specify what happens when you perform various types of mouse clicks on the titlebar, titlebar buttons, or the window of an inactive or active document.

Focus

Settings here determine how a window gets focus (is made active). X allows you to bring a window into focus merely by hovering a mouse over an inactive window—no click required. Some people love this, but it is difficult for former Windows users to become used to this behavior.

Moving

This setting determines how windows behave when you move them, such as displaying contents while moving, or how the window snaps into place when it is released. The two options I frequently set here are settings to display content in moving or resizing windows. When active, these settings cause jaggedness on the display when moving windows and give the visual appearance of a slow or unresponsive system.

Advanced

These settings should really be on other settings pages, but here they are. The shading options affect what happens when you have Shade set for the titlebar double-click action on the Action setting page. I like to Enable Hover so the shade unrolls when I move my mouse over the titlebar. Active desk borders are quite interesting. Basically, with these enabled, you can move your mouse to the edge of a screen and change virtual desktops. For this to work, once set, you need to move your mouse "past" the edge of the screen for at least as long as the millisecond delay you specify here.

Window-Specific Settings

These are the same window geometry settings I covered earlier, with the exception that accessing the settings from this menu choice doesn't automatically import the information you need to identify the window type (application) you want to affect. If you start the process from this dialog, you should click New, then click the Detect button in the window that appears. This setting changes your cursor to a crosshair, and its values are imported when you click on a window. That gets you started, then everything else is the same as before.

Translucency

X has an experimental feature to enable window transparency, meaning that you can see through the window to a limited degree, depending on the opaqueness value you specify here. For this to work, your X server must be configured properly, and for it to work well, you need a 3D accelerated video card. I don't cover how to set up X this way in this book.

KDE offers several keyboard commands to facilitate your use of the desktop. Table 4-2 lists several of the more useful ones. In addition, here are two keyboard and mouse combinations that I've found particularly useful (although it took me a bit of time to train my fingers to use them):

Alt-hold left-mouse button and drag

Perform this action anywhere on a window and you can move it to a new location. This is much quicker than grabbing a window titlebar, and it's useful when you can't reach the titlebar because the window is larger than the screen.

Alt-hold right-mouse button and drag
> Perform this action inside a window to change your pointer to a resizing cursor. Then, simply drag to resize the window. If you perform this action near a corner, you can resize both horizontally and vertically. Using this tip, you can resize a window much more quickly than trying to grab the edge of the window.

Table 4-2. KDE desktop shortcuts

Keyboard shortcut	Action
Alt-F2	Launches a Run Command dialog.
Alt-Tab	Cycles through windows on a desktop.
Alt-Shift-Tab	Reverse-cycles through windows on a desktop.
Alt-F3	Brings up the properties of the active window.
Alt-F4	Closes the active window.
Ctrl-Esc	Brings up the process window (Task Manager to Windows users).
Alt-Ctrl-Esc	Changes your cursor to a skull and crossbones. Click on a window to kill it. Press Esc to cancel the action.
Alt-PrtSc	Creates a screenshot of the active window in PNG format and saves it to the clipboard (Klipper). Press Ctrl-V in the file manager to create a file with the clipboard's content.
Ctrl-PrtSc	Creates a screenshot of the entire active desktop in PNG format and saves it to the clipboard (Klipper). Press Ctrl-V in the file manager to create a file of the clipboard's content.
Alt-F1	Opens the K Menu.
Ctrl-Alt-L	Locks the desktop.
Ctrl-Alt-D	Minimizes all windows to reveal the desktop. Press again to reverse.
Alt-F5	Shows a list of windows on all desktops.
Ctrl-Alt-Insert	Enables Fast User Switching.
Ctrl-Alt-Delete	Logs out.
Ctrl-W	Closes the active child window of an application.
Ctrl-Q	Closes the active application.

Fast User Switching and Sessions

Sometimes other people in your family or workplace need to use your computer. Although you can allow them to work under your login, this isn't very secure. Also, the user might be confused by the way you have configured your desktop or might inadvertently wreck some project you have been working on. It is better to have the user log in as himself. However, doing this doesn't mean that you need to close your applications and log out. Use Fast User Switching instead. This handy feature allows you to keep everything running while someone else logs in, performs his task, and logs off. The menu option for this is K Menu → Switch User, or you can use the keyboard shortcut Ctrl-Alt-Insert. When you run the command, you'll be presented with the choice to:

Start New Session
> Switch to the login screen of a new session.

Lock Current Session
> More secure than the previous option, this one locks your current login so that the person you're allowing on the machine can't switch back to it when you're not around.

Select a Session
> Any existing sessions are listed and you can choose from among them.

KDE also allows you to save sessions so that the next time you log in, everything is brought back to the same state each time. This feature is useful when you want to run the same programs every time you log in and want the application windows to be in specific places. There are two steps to setting this up. First, go to the KDE Control Center and choose KDE Components → Session Manager. Under the On Login grouping, select how you want to configure your sessions. Here are what the choices mean:

Restore previous session
> KDE will save your session state each time you log off. When you log back in, it restores the last saved session.

Restore manually saved session
> With this option enabled, you have to manually choose when to save a session. The option to do this will be made available as K Menu → Save Session. Once you save a session, KDE will restore that session each time you log in. I've found this to be more useful than the previous option.

Start with an empty session
> Enable this if you don't want KDE to save any session data and want to start with an empty desktop each time. You can also use this option to "reset" your sessions if programs you don't want to start continue to do so.

The second step is to set up your desktop the way you want it, and then either save your session manually or simply log off.

File Manager

KDE's file manager is known as Konqueror (which also happens to be its web browser; it's covered in Chapter 5). Konqueror performs all the basic functions you expect from a file manager—namely browsing, moving, copying, deleting files and folders, previewing images and documents, and opening files. Browsing the file manager is as simple as clicking icons. There are also a few toolbar icons, similar to those of a web browser, that let you move forward and back through your previous choices, as well as an Up arrow that lets you move to the directory above your current one.

Konqueror supports context-sensitive right-click menus. The typical menu allows you to Cut, Copy, Paste, Copy To..., Move To..., Delete, and Move to the Trash. In addition, you may have options to open the file with a specific program or a list of programs. If you right-click an archive (zip or tar file), you'll have the choice to extract the items in a few different ways. My personal favorites are the ability to right-click on an ISO image and have the choice to burn it to CD with K3b, and the ability to select multiple files, right-click, and choose to add them to an archive.

Konqueror has a sidebar that provides quick access to many of the features I describe in this section. Press F9 to toggle the sidebar.

Keyboard Commands

The shortcuts Ctrl-C, Ctrl-X, and Ctrl-V work for Copy, Cut, and Paste, respectively. You can also, of course, drag and drop files between file manager windows to move, copy, or link files. Links are pointers to where the real files are (like shortcuts in Windows) and are handy ways to access a single file from multiple directories. Table 4-3 shows some keyboard shortcuts that can be combined with the drag-and-drop action to bypass the menu that pops up when you drop a file or directory.

Table 4-3. Keyboard and mouse combinations for manipulating files

Keyboard shortcut	Action
Ctrl-drag	Copies to the new location automatically.
Shift-drag	Moves to the new location automatically.
Ctrl-Shift-drag	Creates a link at the new location automatically.
Ctrl-Alt-drag	Opens a dialog to rename the file when you drop it.

Configuring Konqueror

Konqueror's default window (in file manager mode) is usually a frame that displays the files of a single directory as large icons. This appearance can be customized and made to stick, once you know a few things about configuring Konqueror.

First off, Konqueror (both the file manager and web browser) uses profiles to remember custom settings. Without saving changes to a profile, Konqueror won't even remember its window size the next time you open it. Profiles are configured through the Konqueror menu Settings → Save View Profile "*ProfileName*." There are two checkboxes: one to save the window size, the other to save the location. You can create more profiles as needed by typing in a new name for the profile and saving it. I'll show you why this is useful in just a bit.

Second, Konqueror supports different ways of viewing the file icons. This feature is controlled from the View menu—specifically the View Mode, Icon Size, and Show Details submenus. Play around with these to see which settings you like.

Finally, Konqueror windows can be split into multiple frames using keyboard commands (Ctrl-Shift-L for vertical splits and Ctrl-Shift-T for horizontal ones) or options on the Windows menu. Multiple frames allow you to view different parts of the filesystem at the same time, making file management easier.

You can combine each of these customization features in myriad ways. For example, you can create a profile that displays a hierarchal view of the entire filesystem, with a horizontally split view on the right, your home directory on top, and whatever directories you are currently browsing on the bottom. Use these directions as a template to create your own useful profiles:

1. Open a Konqueror window and size it to your desired dimensions.

2. Press Ctrl-Shift-L to split the main window vertically.

3. Click on the righthand frame and press Ctrl-Shift-T to split that frame horizontally. Resize the frames as you see fit.

4. Click on each frame and browse to the location you want to view in that frame by default.

5. Set the view properties you want for each frame (i.e., the settings under View Mode, Icon Size, and Show Details).

6. Click on the vertical plane on the left, and choose View → Lock to Current Location.

7. Look in the lower-left corner of each frame. You'll see a small box next to the status bar for that frame. When you click this box, it displays a small "chain." Click this box for the vertical frame and the bottom horizontal one. This links these two views so the horizontal frame will display the contents of whichever folder you click on in the vertical one.

8. Click Settings → Save View Profile to save your settings. Be sure to give this a unique name, and leave the boxes to save window size and window URLs checked. For this example, I've named my profile "Power Browsing."

There are several ways to access the profile that you just created. The simplest is to open Konqueror, click Settings → Load View Profile, and select your profile. This way is slightly inconvenient if you plan to use this profile frequently. Another option is to add a button to your panel to access any profile. To do this, right-click the K Menu icon and choose Panel Menu → Add to Panel → Special Button → Konqueror Profiles. Quite handy.

A third option is to create an icon that launches a specific profile:

1. Right-click on your desktop and choose Create New → Link to Application.

2. Give your new link a name in the dialog box that appears. You can also give it a custom icon by clicking the icon in the dialog and making a new selection.

3. Click the Application tab and, in the Command field, type the following: `kfmclient openProfile "Power Browsing"`

4. Save your changes. Place the icon wherever you want within your filesystem, or add it to the panel by dragging it there.

In step 3, `kfmclient` is the command-line name for Konqueror, `openProfile` is an option this command takes that tells it which profile to start with, and `"Power Browsing"` is the name of the profile I created earlier (you should put in your own profile name). The quotes are needed only if your profile name has a space in it.

You can create as many profiles as you find useful. These techniques also come in handy when using Konqueror as a web browser, except that then you might be more interested in multiple tabs than split views.

Protocol Handlers

You can use Konqueror to browse remote filesystems using a variety of protocols, just by typing a special command known as a protocol handler in the Location field. Table 4-4 lists several of the file access protocols you might want to try out. Though this is not as convenient as the automatic network browsing in Microsoft Windows, it is ultimately more flexible and powerful because it is not limited to only the Server Message Block (SMB) protocol. These protocol handlers can also be entered into any KDE Save or Open dialog. Some of these protocols may require secondary software to be installed—a warning message will tell you what you are missing. Each of these options, besides smb://, require you to supply a hostname or IP address.

Table 4-4. Protocol handlers for remote filesystems

Protocol handler	Use to
sftp://	Access a remote system.
fish://	Access a system with a running SSH server and Perl installed.
ftp://	Access a remote system.
smb://	Access remote SMB filesystems, such as those found on a Windows network.
nfs://	Access a remote system.
webdav://	Access WebDAV shared resources.

After connecting a remote filesystem, you can create a bookmark to that location and reuse it in the future. You do this just as you create a bookmark to a web page, by clicking Bookmarks → Add Bookmark or using the keyboard shortcut Ctrl-B.

The usefulness of the protocol handlers is not limited to accessing remote filesystems. Table 4-5 reveals several more protocols you might want to try. Pay particular attention to the audiocd:/ handler—it's darn useful.

Table 4-5. Other KDE protocol handlers

Protocol handler	Use to
audiocd:/	Rip a CD directly from the file manager.
man:/	Browse and read manpages (manual pages) inside Konqueror. Great for printing manpages.
system:/	View the next four protocol handlers.
remote:/	Access a few ways to browse the local network.

Table 4-5. Other KDE protocol handlers (continued)

Protocol handler	Use to
settings:/	Access icons to launch various portions of the Control Center.
media:/	Access attached storage devices. Great for USB memory keys.
trash:/	Access your trash folder.
print:/	View several printer and print queue management tools.
zeroconf:/	Browse the network for other zeroconf, Rendezvous, or Bonjour clients.

Special mention goes to the zeroconf:/ protocol handler, which lets you browse for zero configuration (also known as Rendezvous or Bonjour) resources on your local network. This is still an experimental feature in KDE, but it already allows you to access remote filesystems, play network games (like kbattleship), and connect to remote systems allowing VNC or remote desktop connections (look under K Menu → System → Remote Desktop Sharing to find out more about this feature).

The KDE Menu

This menu is usually represented by an icon in the lower-left corner of the screen. As with the Windows XP Start button, clicking this icon displays the KDE menu, which contains launchers for the most commonly used programs, as well as links to various control panels, special utilities, and the option to log off the system.

You can control what is on the menu by using KDE's menu editing tool or one provided specifically by your distribution. The KDE tool is easy to access: right-click the menu icon and choose Menu Editor, which launches a menu configuration program.

Using this program is straightforward. The groupings and items that make up the menu are on the left side, and on the right is a properties page for each item that you select on the left. The changes you make here apply to your menu only—no one else's. You can add, move, and delete groupings and individual items. Click on an individual item to see how its properties page is filled out, then use that as a template for creating your own items.

On the properties page for a menu item, you'll notice a "Current shortcut key" option. Click the None button to open a window where you can enter the shortcut. This dialog expects you to "perform" your shortcut, starting with a modifier key (Ctrl, Shift, or Alt), and followed by one or more other keys or further additional modifiers. Once you've made your shortcut and saved it, you can launch the program using that key sequence.

Mandriva does not respect the changes you make in the menu editing program (though it should respect the shortcut key you define). Mandriva's menu editing program, called Menudrake, is found under K Menu → System → Configuration → Other → Menudrake. Edits to this menu affect the current user only. To change menus for all users, run the program as root from the Mandrake Control Center and choose the System menu.

The KDE Control Center

KDE comes with its own control panel that is independent of any that may be provided by your distribution. That said, many distributions customize the KDE Control Center to better suit their sensibilities pertaining to where particular options should be stored. In most instances, you can launch the control panel by clicking K Menu → Control Center. If the option doesn't exist on the main menu, look for it on an administrative or system submenu. Alternatively, you can launch the Run Command dialog by pressing Alt-F2 and typing **kcontrol**.

Using the KDE Control Center, you can access most of the customization options allowed by KDE. The control center is easy to use. Configuration panels are accessed from a list on the left that is conveniently grouped by topic. (Actually, it attempts to be so grouped; many people complain that the Control Center is needlessly complex.) Expand a group and click an item on the list to access the configuration.

There are perhaps thousands of things that can be configured in the Control Center, but, for many users, the defaults are good enough and you won't change them. Here, I describe the configuration panels that I believe you'll be most interested in.

TIP

The location and names of some of these items vary depending upon your distribution. For example, in Mandriva, the Appearance group is labeled LookNFeel.

Appearance and Themes → Background
> Allows you to set the wallpaper for your desktop. Using the "Settings for Desktop" drop-down list, you can set different wallpaper for each desktop. You can also access this configuration panel by right-clicking on the desktop and choosing Configure Desktop.

Appearance and Themes → Screen Saver
> Allows you to choose and configure your screensavers. It's also accessible by right-clicking your desktop and choosing Configure Desktop.

Appearance and Themes → Colors
> In this window, you can set the colors used by the windows, menus, and widgets in KDE. ("Widget" is just a term used to describe things like buttons, scrollbars, checkboxes, and other standard elements of the GUI.)

Appearance and Themes → Fonts

> Here you can quickly choose which fonts and font sizes to use for toolbars, menus, and icons. You can also enable KDE's support for anti-aliasing here.

Appearance and Themes → Icons

> In this area, you can select your preferred icon set. An icon set is a group of icons that share a common look. By selecting a new icon set, you can quickly change the look of all the icons on your desktop and in program toolbars.

Appearance and Themes → Splash Screen

> Here you can determine the look of your login screen. Select a screen from the list and click Apply. Click Test to see a simulation of what that screen looks like while loading.

Appearance and Themes → Style

> In this panel, you can set the shape and size of buttons, scrollbars, tabs, lists, and checkboxes. (A Style defines the way widgets look.) Styles can enable effects like transparency and fade for menus.

Desktop → Multiple Desktops

> Use this configuration panel to add, remove, and name virtual desktops. It's also accessible by right-clicking on your desktop and choosing Configure Desktop.

KDE Components → File Associations

> Use this configuration panel to set your preferences for which program will open which file type (MIME type). The items you add to the Application Preference Order list determine which programs appear on the right-click Open With... option. An alternative way to set these is to right-click on a file, choose Properties, then click on the wrench icon.

Peripherals → Display
> Here you can set the resolution, color depth, and refresh rate for your display. These settings go into effect when you start KDE. See the section "X," in Chapter 7, for more information about these settings.

Peripherals → Printers
> Use this panel to add new printers or configure existing ones. I provide more information on printers in Chapter 7.

Regional & Accessibility → Country/Region & Language
> Here you'll find settings to configure how KDE handles dates, numbers, and currency.

Regional & Accessibility → Keyboard Layout
> Configure the keyboard layout for your language.

Regional & Accessibility → Keyboard Shortcuts
> A very useful configuration panel to configure keyboard shortcuts to launch programs or configure actions within programs.

Security & Privacy → KDE Wallet
> Use KDE wallet to have the system remember your passwords for you.

Sound & Multimedia → Audio CDs
> This configuration panel specifies the filenames and encoding settings to be used when ripping music CDs from Konqueror.

System Administration → Login Manager
> Access the Administrator Mode on this panel to configure how the KDM login manager (introduced in Chapter 2) looks and behaves.

As you can see, KDE is a highly configurable desktop environment. The web site *http://www.kde-look.org* is a one-stop location for all things related to KDE's appearance. Here you'll find wallpapers, icon sets, styles, themes, and window decorations that can help you create a very personalized KDE desktop.

## CHAPTER 5

Applications

Linux enthusiasts are often told that Linux will never take off on the desktop until there are more applications that run on it. Although I understand what these critics mean, I often wonder if they are truly aware of the diversity and usefulness of Linux programs that are already available. If you can identify the narrow range of functionality you really need from a computer, whether for business or personal use, you may find that Linux and open source software can meet your needs.

The problem is finding which programs, among the thousands available, best meet your requirements. Though there is no replacement for doing actual program testing yourself, I can help you get started by showing you many of the most popular programs available. If your needs extend beyond the types of programs presented here, I suggest you start your search at the Freshmeat (*http://www.freshmeat.net*) and Sourceforge (*http://www.sourceforge.net*) web sites; both are searchable archives for thousands of open source programs, and they are valuable resources when looking for a task-specific program. In addition, there are also GNOME and KDE web sites that have extensive lists of software favored by these desktop environments. Here are a few of these sites:

> *http://www.gnomefiles.org*
> *http://www.kde-apps.org*
> *http://www.kde-files.org*

When possible in this chapter, I've tried to present at least two programs for each program type. One will integrate nicely with GNOME, and the other is either part of KDE or is made to integrate with it. Of course, all of these programs will run under the other desktop environment—they just might not look as nice, or they may take longer to load.

With most distributions, you can install the program using the appropriate package manager command followed by the program name. If you can't find the right name for the program, use the package manager search feature I've provided in Chapter 6.

Many of the programs in this chapter are focused on multimedia. There is no surprise, as a desktop computer is used just as frequently for entertainment as it is for work. To learn more about the multimedia capabilities of Linux, read *Linux Multimedia Hacks* (O'Reilly).

Web Browsers

There are a plethora of web browsers for Linux. Though you won't be using Microsoft's Internet Explorer or Apple's Safari, you will find plenty of other browsers that offer just as many features, if not more. Their basic use is the same with other browsers, such as Internet Explorer, so I won't bore you with simple usage instructions.

In each of these browsers, you'll have the ability to use tabs, which offer a convenient way to visit multiple sites without cluttering your screen with browser windows. You're probably already familiar with tabs in some configuration windows. When you click on a tab at the top of the window, the configuration window box stays the same size and in the same place, but the available options change inside that box. Tabs in browsers work the same way, except that instead of configuration options, each tab holds a new web page. Once you try this feature out, I know you'll learn to love it.

Firefox

http://www.mozilla.org

Firefox is based upon code from the Mozilla browser. It is a successful attempt to create a leaner, faster-loading, and more simplistic browser that is actually a pleasure to use. In addition to tabs, pop-up ad blocking (it's one of the best browsers at this), and themes, Firefox can be improved by loading community-developed extensions. These applets provide additional functions—such as Flash ad blocking, controls for your favorite media player, and weather updates—and they can turn your browser into an RSS reader (explained a little later in this section). Firefox will run on Linux, Windows, and Mac OS X, and it has rapidly become the preferred alternative to Internet Explorer.

To add extensions to Firefox, click Tools → Extensions. In the dialog that appears, click the Get More Extensions link in the lower right to open a web page where you can browse for and install new extensions. You can use this same dialog to update or remove extensions.

Firefox supports Really Simple Syndication (RSS) feeds. These feeds bring the Web to you by telling you when pages have been updated, instead of you having to visit the site to find out. A web site that supports RSS displays a small, orange icon in the lower-right corner of the browser window. Click this icon to reveal a menu choice to subscribe to that RSS feed. When you click this icon, the Add Bookmark dialog appears and you can choose where to put this subscription link. After you've done so, go to your bookmarks and you'll see a new submenu entry, the contents of which are the "articles" of the RSS feed. This is RSS at its most basic. To increase Firefox's RSS ability, I suggest you install the Sage extension.

Though Firefox has a nifty search bar in the top-right corner, I find that I don't use it that much. I've become accustomed to the web shortcuts I use in Konqueror (read the upcoming "Konqueror" section to learn more about web shortcuts), and I want to perform my searches from the regular location field. The technical reviewer for this book pointed out that Firefox has a similar function as Konqueror, but you have to set it up manually.

To do this, visit a web page that has a search field; for example, at Urban Dictionary (*http://www.urbandictionary.com*), you can look up user-contributed definitions of slang terms. Right-click on the search field and choose "Add a Keyword for this Search." In the dialog that appears, give the search a name and memorable shortcut sequence (I used ud for this search). Click Add to save the search. To use the saved search, just type your shortcut in the location bar, followed by a space, and the term you want to search for. Press Enter, and Firefox will execute your special search without needing to visit the web page first!

I'm a big fan of keyboard shortcuts, and Firefox has a lot of useful ones. I've picked my favorites and put them in Table 5-1.

Table 5-1. Firefox keyboard shortcuts on Linux

Keyboard shortcut	Action
Ctrl-W	Closes the application or the active tab.
Ctrl-T	Creates a new tab.
Ctrl-click link	Opens a link in a new tab.
Ctrl-N	Opens a new browser window.
Alt-D or Ctrl-L	Places the cursor in the address field and highlights any text found there.
Ctrl-+	Increases font size.
Ctrl- -	Decreases font size.
Ctrl-0	Restores font size to the default.
Ctrl-K	Places the cursor in the search field and highlights any text found there.
Ctrl-PgDn	Moves through tabs from left to right.

Table 5-1. Firefox keyboard shortcuts on Linux (continued)

Keyboard shortcut	Action
Ctrl-PgUp	Moves through tabs from right to left.
Ctrl-0	Restores font to default size.
Ctrl-D	Adds a bookmark for the current page.
Alt-left arrow	Goes back a page.
Alt-right arrow	Goes forward a page.
Ctrl-F	Opens find field at the bottom of the screen.
F11	Toggles full-screen mode.
Up and Down arrows	Scrolls a web page one line at a time.
PgUp and PgDn	Scrolls a web page one full screen at a time.

Firefox is designed to be simple to use and configure, which is why the toolbars and configuration menus have only the basic options. But, just for kicks, take a look under Firefox's skin sometime and see all the options that are actually available. To do this, type **about:config** in the address field and press Enter.

If you're interested in learning more about Firefox, I suggest reading *Firefox Hacks* (O'Reilly).

Konqueror

http://konqueror.kde.org

KDE provides its own web browser: Konqueror. The browser provides tabs and pop-up ad blocking, and it is Netscape plug-in compatible. Konqueror loads very quickly and is reasonably fast at displaying most web pages. However, its rendering engine KHTML is not as sophisticated as Mozilla's Gecko, and you will occasionally run into web sites that do not display correctly or that load extremely slowly. Although you can run Konqueror under GNOME, doing so costs you its main benefit—quick loading.

Konqueror is installed when you install KDE, and, in fact, it's the same program as the Konqueror file manager covered in Chapter 4. You can use the Konqueror profile information from the file manager section to create your own web browser profiles. This feature is particularly useful when you have a collection of web sites you visit frequently and want to load each web site in a separate tab. To set this up, load the web sites into their own tabs, then save a new profile. Later, when you access this profile, all of those tabs and web sites are loaded automatically. Don't save these multiple tabs in your default Web Browsing profile, or these web sites will load every time you launch Konqueror.

TIP

Tabs in Konqueror are particularly versatile because you can mix web pages, FTP sites, local and remote file-systems all in the same window.

Table 5-2 lists keyboard shortcuts that will make your browsing experience more enjoyable.

Table 5-2. Konqueror keyboard shortcuts

Keyboard shortcut	Action
Ctrl-Shift-N or Ctrl-T	Creates a new tab.
Ctrl-N	Opens a new browser window.
Ctrl-W	Closes the active tab.
Ctrl-Q	Closes the browser window.
Alt-left arrow	Goes back a page.
Alt-right arrow	Goes forward a page.
Ctrl-R or F5	Reloads a page.
Ctrl-left click	Opens the link in a new tab.
Page Down	Scrolls down one screen.
Page Up	Scrolls up one screen.

Table 5-2. Konqueror keyboard shortcuts (continued)

Keyboard shortcut	Action
Alt-0	Places the cursor in the Location field and highlights the text.
Ctrl-[	Moves to the browser tab to the left of your current one.
Ctrl-]	Moves to the browser tab to the right of your current one.

Perhaps my favorite feature of Konqueror are the web shortcuts that you can access from the Location field (same as the Address or URL field in other browsers). A web shortcut is a shorthand way of telling Konqueror to access the search features of a particular web site and apply the search string you type in. For example, to search Google for information about genealogy, enter this string: **gg:genealogy**. The gg stands for Google. Another example is a search of the Internet Movie Database (*http://imdb.com*) for Jimmy Stewart: **imdb:Jimmy Stewart**. To see a list of web shortcuts that Konqueror supports, click Settings → Configure Konqueror, then click the Web Shortcuts link on the left.

Email

Though Linux has dozens of email clients, only a few of the graphical ones have risen to the top and become truly popular. Discussed here are Thunderbird, Evolution, and Kontact. These programs often mimic the look, feel, and features of their Windows counterparts (Eudora, Outlook Express, and Outlook), but they are not without innovative features of their own.

Each of these email clients runs a configuration wizard when you first launch it. To take advantage of this, be prepared to enter your email account information, such as the names of your POP3, IMAP, or SMTP mail servers, and your username and password.

Each of these email clients can use the same method to store email—the traditional mbox format—which means that you can freely change between these clients without having to import or export your mail each time. To make this work, point each client to the same email storage folder, which is usually called *Mail* and is located in your home directory. Kontact, by default, will create new folders in the newer maildir format, but it will read existing mbox folders just fine, and you can always force a new folder to use mbox so that it will be compatible with the other email clients.

Evolution and Kontact both have a similar feature that is called "virtual folders" in the former and "saved searches" in the latter. This feature is similar to mail filters except that they don't actually move your email messages around. Instead, messages that match the specified criteria are placed virtually in the search folder, where you can access them, act upon them, and even delete them. By "virtually," I mean that the messages that appear in the search folder are really stored in the originating folder, like your Inbox, and you're seeing only a link to that message. When the search criteria is no longer true, the message no longer appears in the search folder, but the original stays in the originating folder.

What good are these types of searches? Well, using this feature, you can create a folder that displays only unread messages from your boss, or one that shows only messages about a specific project that were sent from a particular person, or messages that you marked as urgent regardless of the folder they exist in.

WARNING

Deleting a message in a virtual folder will also delete it in its originating folder.

Thunderbird

http://www.mozilla.org/products/thunderbird

This email client is based upon code from the Mozilla Mail program. It is cross-platform and runs on Linux, Windows, and Mac OS X. Think of it as the open source equivalent to Outlook Express, as it provides all the basic email functions, an address book, and a newsgroup reader.

Like Firefox, Thunderbird also supports extensions to give it increased functionality. There are not as many as for Firefox, but, given time, I'm sure you'll see a lot of useful ones pop up. Thunderbird already includes a statistical spam filter that improves its accuracy as you train it. The training is simple: you merely mark a message as Junk or Not Junk, and with enough time and email, the accuracy rate of identifying spam increases dramatically.

Evolution

http://www.gnome.org/projects/evolution/

Evolution is one of the most popular email clients on Linux. It is very similar to Microsoft Outlook in both its looks and capabilities, and with the Novell Connector, it can even be configured to interoperate with a Microsoft Exchange groupware server. Since version 2.0, it has also included native support for Novell's Groupwise.

Evolution supports POP and IMAP, and it comes with an organizer, contact manager, and to-do list manager.

As I discussed at the beginning of this section, Evolution supports virtual folders (vFolder). If you want to filter on the Subject, Sender, Recipients, or Mailing List of a message, the quick way to get started is to right-click on a message that you want to capture, choose Create Rule From Message, and choose one of the vFolder options. A new window will open and you can name the rule and add additional criteria. You also need to specify which mail folders you want the vFolder rules to scan. Once you're done and click OK, the vFolder is created in the folder list and you can click on it to see the results.

Like Thunderbird, Evolution has a built-in spam detector that you can improve upon through training. Simply mark spam messages as junk, and periodically view your Junk folder and mark any nonspam messages as not-junk.

The Contact, Calendar, and Task modules of Evolution are quite nice and feel very integrated into the application. In all, I would say this application has the most polish of all the email clients and most feels like it can handle the tasks a Microsoft Outlook user wants to perform.

I won't go into keyboard shortcuts for this program because Evolution provides a handy quick reference card right from the Help menu that contains all the shortcuts you need.

Kontact

http://kontact.kde.org

Kontact is a collection of several independent KDE programs that provide email (KMail), contact management (KAddress-book), an organizer and to-do list (KOrganizer), a news-group reader (KNode), and an RSS reader (Akregator). By combining these programs into one interface, the KDE group has created a viable alternative to Microsoft Outlook and Evolution.

Though Kontact can integrate with the open source group-ware server Kroupware, it doesn't support any special interoperability with a Microsoft Exchange Server, other than simple email retrieval via POP or IMAP.

With most distributions, Kontact is a part of the KDE PIM package. Ubuntu provides it as a separate download.

Table 5-3 lists the keyboard shortcuts, which will quickly turn you into a KMail power user. The other modules in Kontact have their own keyboard commands (though some of them, like Ctrl-N, are shared); consult the applications' help files to learn those.

Table 5-3. KMail keyboard shortcuts

Keyboard shortcut	Action
Ctrl-N	Creates a new email message.
R	Replies to the message highlighted in the message list.
A	Replies to all recipients and the sender of the message highlighted in the message list.
F	Forwards the message highlighted in the message list as an attachment.
Shift-F	Forwards the message highlighted in the message list as inline text.
Ctrl-A	Selects all the messages in the message list.
Right arrow or N	Moves down through the message list.
Left arrow or P	Moves up through the message list.
Up and down arrows	Moves up and down through a message shown in the preview pane.
+	Goes to the next unread message in the current folder.
–	Goes to a previous unread message in the current folder.
Shift-left arrow and Shift-right arrow	Selects multiple messages in the message list.
Space	Advances through a message in the preview pane. If you are already at the bottom of a message, this will take you to the next unread message in the current folder.
Ctrl-+	Goes to the next folder that contains an unread message.
Ctrl-–	Goes to a previous folder that contains an unread message.
Ctrl-left arrow	Moves up the folder list.
Ctrl-right arrow	Moves down the folder list.
Ctrl-space	Opens a folder you've moved to.
Ctrl-J	Applies any manual filters to the current folder.

Like most email applications, KMail supports the ability to filter your email to send it to folders or perform an action on it. Here this feature is accessed through the Settings → Configure Filters menu. Create a new filter, enter the criteria, and save. The order of the filters in the column on the left of this screen determines the order in which filters are applied. In most cases, when a message matches a particular filter, it is not checked against the filters further down the list.

As I covered in the introduction to this section, KMail has a saved searches feature. You can access this feature from the normal search window (press S or click the magnifying glass icon on the toolbar). The difference between a saved search and regular search is that to create the former, you enter a name in the "Search folder name" field. Once this is done and you've run the search, a new folder appears in your folder listing at the bottom, under the grouping Searches. Click this to access the results of the saved search.

KMail has an antispam wizard that can detect antispam programs installed on your computer and help you set them up. This approach creates a very flexible solution that doesn't force a particular spam-catching method on you.

Here are brief descriptions of some of the remaining Kontact applications:

KOrganizer
> This program provides the calendar and reminder functions of Kontact. You can also run this as a standalone program. In order for the reminder function to work, you must be running the KAlarm daemon, which is usually configured properly by the distributions and is represented in your system tray by a small calendar with a hand bell.

KAddressbook (Contacts)
> Entries that you make in KAddressbook can be accessed from KMail, which saves you a lot of time typing email addresses. In addition, the contact files hold a lot of useful information like addresses, phone numbers, web sites, and birth and anniversary dates. These dates can also be displayed in KOrganizer by adding the KAddressbook Birthdays resource (click Add in the Calendar box in KOrganizer's lower-left corner).

KNode (News)
> This is a very powerful newsgroup reader that lets you easily maintain different identities for each newsgroup you read.

Akregator (Feeds)
> This is KDE's RSS feed reader. You can add new feeds through Konqueror by right-clicking the orange RSS icon that appears in the lower right of RSS enabled sites and choose to add the feed to Akregator. This is a new program, just added in KDE 3.4, so expect its features to improve rapidly in the next year.

Instant Messaging and IRC

If you have teenagers, then you know that their social lives live and die by their cell phones and ability to instant message with their friends. Linux has two great IM programs in Gaim and Kopete, both of which allow you to access multiple networks at the same time. This means that you can be on the MSN, AOL, and Yahoo! networks all from one client, and have full capability to chat with anyone you know.

Gaim

http://gaim.sourceforge.net

Gaim is a multiprotocol chat client that integrates particularly well with a GNOME desktop.

Gaim is the oldest of the IM clients on Linux and probably the most widely used. It supports several protocols, including MSN, AOL, Yahoo!, Jabber, Napster, ICQ, IRC, and Novell Groupwise. If any of your machines still run Windows and you want a free multiprotocol IM client, then try out the Windows port of Gaim.

I'm not familiar with the current chat offerings on Windows, but Gaim supports the same ones I used in the past, such as: buddy pounce, smilies, away messages, file transfers, embedded images, and user icons.

The interface is not particularly remarkable, but it is highly functional and easy to figure out for any IM user. Each conversation can have its own window or can exist as tabs in a single one. Check out Tools → Preferences for more options like these. Pay particular attention to the Plugins settings in the Preferences window: several of these are particularly useful.

Kopete

http://kopete.kde.org

Kopete is the multiprotocol chat client that comes with KDE. It's a lot like Gaim, except that it is designed to be part of KDE. As is typical for a KDE application, there are a lot of configuration options to twiddle with. These can be found under Settings → Configure Kopete. If you're a long-time user of another chat program, you should look at the options under the Chat Window tab of the Appearance configuration screen. Here you can choose a style of chat that most looks like what you are used to.

Protocol support in Kopete is the same as those mentioned for Gaim; however, Kopete also supports sending SMS text messages, which can be sent to cell phones.

There are two things that have caused me hang-ups with Kopete. First, you don't log onto a network; instead, you change your status to be Online. This is done from the File menu, from the toolbar icon for Status, or by using the icon in the lower-right corner of the buddy window. Second, you can't start a chat with someone who is not in your contacts.

Office Suites

For most people, there is really only one office suite that matters: Microsoft Office. However, outside the mainstream where everyone is dependent upon the need to open and share Word and Excel documents, there are dozens of office suites that are perfect for personal use—some of which provide limited ability to collaborate with MS Office users.

The big hang-up with these alternative office suites is not their features or ease of use, but their imperfect ability to open MS Office-formatted documents and to save to that format. Although the data of the file is always intact, formatting, formulas, tracked changes, and macros often get lost in translation.

OpenOffice.org

http://www.openoffice.org

The best known of the alternative office suites is OpenOffice. org (OOo)—also sold by Sun Microsystems as StarOffice.

OOo runs on Linux, Solaris, Windows, and, to a limited extent, on Mac OS X. This office suite is the best one at importing and exporting Microsoft Office documents, and it also comes the closest to matching MS Office's capabilities.

In fact, in some ways, it even exceeds the capabilities of MS Office; for example, its ability to handle longer documents without crashing or corrupting the files, its more powerful styles for easier document formatting, and its truly easy-to-use headers and footers.

There are several components to this office suite. Here are descriptions of the most important ones:

Writer/Web

This is a word processing program. You can use Writer to create all kinds of documents, from simple letters or résumés to complex documents, such as books or a college thesis. Writer includes a component (Web) that lets you create web pages of mid-level complexity.

Calc

This spreadsheet program is a very capable replacement for Excel. It supports hundreds of functions to perform complex calculations, charting, and integration with outside data sources. Although it has its own macro language, it cannot run Excel macros.

Impress

This is a presentation program. Impress allows you to create presentations in a similar manner to PowerPoint. It lacks PowerPoint's diversity of effects, but it is still capable of creating very nice presentations. One interesting feature is that you can save presentations to a Flash file, which lets you put your presentations on the Web easily.

Base

This is a new feature for the 2.0 version of OOo. Base is a database application, similar to Microsoft Access. It provides a graphical way to create and manage your own databases.

KOffice

http://koffice.kde.org

The KDE developers have created their own complete office suite, KOffice.

KOffice is not as feature rich as OOo, nor does it do as good a job at importing Microsoft Office files. But, it is actively developed and getting better at these tasks all the time. KOffice does integrate nicely into the rest of KDE, loads quickly, and provides quick access to the functions you're likely to use most.

In addition to the typical office suite functions, KOffice includes a vector drawing program, a diagram program similar to Visio, a tool to generate and format reports, and a project planning tool similar to Microsoft Project.

Microsoft Office

http://www.codeweavers.com

I'm not out of my mind for listing Microsoft Office as a Linux office suite! By using the CodeWeavers CrossOver Office product, you can even run Microsoft Office on Linux. It works best with Office 2000 and higher versions, for which you must have a license and provide the install CD.

You can obtain a trial version of CrossOver Office from *http://www.codeweavers.com/products/download_trial/* or purchase it directly from the CodeWeavers web site.

This product works with a minimum of fuss and without excess use of system resources. I've personally used it only for running Microsoft Office 2000, but it runs nearly flawlessly and behaves just as the application would natively perform on Windows. In fact, the most glaring bug I've come across is the side scrollbar disappearing on newly opened documents. As soon as you minimize and then restore the window (or resize it in any way), the bar always comes back.

Other Windows programs can be run with CrossOver Office. Visit the CodeWeavers web site to learn more.

Video Players

There are dozens of applications for playing movies and videos on Linux. Most of these are merely frontends to the two playback engines: MPlayer and xine. These engines do all of the heavy lifting, such as decoding the video and audio and sending it to the display and soundcard. But, increasingly, users are finding that they don't need to interact with the engines directly because the frontends provided with their distribution provide all the features they really need.

The trick to getting all of this to work is installing all the codecs, which are the pieces of software that decode the various media types so you can play them back. Visit *http://www.mplayerhq.hu* to get a package of codecs that should give you everything you need. Just click the Download link and then download the essential codecs package. Open the downloaded archive and copy the contents to */usr/lib/win32/*. Both MPlayer and xine should look for the codecs there, which means that the two programs I describe next should be able to play back most media types.

TIP

Newer versions of MPlayer look for the codecs in */usr/local/lib/codecs/* or */usr/lib/codecs/*, but xine isn't looking for them there yet. By the time you read this book, you may be able to place the files there.

In addition to installing the codecs, you may need to replace your distro's version of MPlayer or xine. Many distro's cripple these programs so that they can't play certain formats, even if you have the correct codecs installed. In Chapter 6, I tell you how to add new software repositories to your package management program and download third-party software. Find a multimedia repository for your distribution, add it, and install updated versions of MPlayer and xine to fix playback problems. In some cases, I've provided the location of a repository that you can use.

Kaffeine

http://kaffeine.sourceforge.net

Kaffeine is a KDE frontend to the xine video player. As such, it is capable of playing back all of the media formats that xine can handle.

There is nothing particularly difficult or special to the use of Kaffeine. Insert your media, launch the application, and watch. Playback controls are standard and the program configuration options are very limited. Under Settings → Configure xine, you can set many of the parameters that control the backend. Some distributions hide a few options until you click Expert Options in the configuration window.

Kaffeine will integrate with Konqueror to enable media playback within your browser window. This is very convenient for the playback of streaming video and audio files. The playback features are very limited until you install the codecs package mentioned earlier.

Some distros run a wizard when you first launch Kaffeine. This wizard may give you useful information about installing the codecs or obtaining the non-crippled version of xine.

Totem

http://www.gnome.org/projects/totem/

Totem is another frontend for the xine player, although it can also use the new GStreamer library (which is a very new backend for multimedia playback). If your distro has built Totem with GStreamer as the default playback engine, then you may need to install additional gst-plug-ins (available through your package manager) to play most video and audio formats.

As you can tell from that URL, Totem is a GNOME application and looks most at home on that desktop. It can, of course, be used in KDE; some distros, such as Mandriva, prefer Totem over Kaffeine, despite their emphasis on the KDE desktop.

Like Kaffeine, there is nothing particularly remarkable about the Totem interface. The application can be figured out easily with just a couple of minutes of clicking on the menus.

Music Ripping, Encoding, and Playing

Linux users love their music as much as the next person—or more—which is probably why so many developers have spent so much programming time on music applications, like the ones listed here.

Grip

http://nostatic.org/grip/

Using Grip, you can quickly rip your music CDs and convert the files to MP3, Ogg, FLAC, or other formats.

This program is nothing short of amazing in its ability to rip CDs the way you want. Grip can look up your album information on the Web, rip partial selections from a track, tag the tracks the way you specify—as well as store them in a user-defined directory structure—and make use of multiple processors for encoding. It comes with a built-in music player, but I must admit I've seldom used it for that.

Although Grip fits in best in a GNOME desktop, it is worth taking a look at, even if you run KDE or another desktop environment.

KAudioCreator

http://www.icefox.net/programs/?program=KAudioCreator

What GRIP does for GNOME users, KAudioCreator does for KDE users.

In a strange twist, this program is actually more simplistic than its GNOME counterpart, Grip. Beyond choosing which encoder to use, the most complicated procedure is using the wizard to create the command that tells the program what directory structure to create to store a ripped track in.

Konqueror

http://konqueror.kde.org

In case you missed my brief coverage of the feature in Chapter 4, Konqueror can rip CDs for you. Just place your CD in the drive, wait a few seconds, and then go to the URL audiocd:/, and you'll see files and folders representing the music on your CD. To rip the music, drag the files to a location on your hard drive.

TIP

Alternatively, you can get to the CD files by opening the Konqueror sidebar (F9), expanding Services, and choosing the Audio CD Browser option.

The files in the root of the CD are in the WAV format; the directories each represent a different format you can rip to. Please note: these files aren't pre-encoded and sitting on the CD—the folders are just convenient ways for you to specify what type of encoding you want when you copy the files over. You must have a suitable encoder installed for each type to work. Ogg is installed by default for most distributions, but MP3 and FLAC support may need to be added. The Full CD folder has images of all the music in different encoded formats.

The settings that control the quality of the encoding can be found in the KDE Control Center under Sound & Multimedia → Audio CDs.

amaroK

http://amarok.kde.org

amaroK is a KDE-based music collection management tool and player.

I have to admit that I love this little program because it got me out of a rut of listening to the same albums time and again and reinterested me in all of my music collection. It did this through its ability to tie into the web server Audioscrobbler, its automatic lyric fetching, and its rule-based playlist creation ability.

If you're not familiar with it, Audioscrobbler (*http://www.audioscrobbler.com*) is a site where you can register and report your music-listening habits. Well, actually, your music-playing application reports what music you listen to. Most do this through a downloaded plug-in, but amaroK has the ability built in. Audioscrobbler then matches up your listening habits with those of other people who listen to the same music. It then makes suggestions as to which music in your collection should be played next. amaroK can be configured to automatically add these picks to your current playlist.

In addition, Audioscrobbler recommends new artists based upon the tastes of people who listen to similar music as you. This is a great way to find out about new music you might otherwise never know existed. And amaroK makes this all seamless, once you enable the feature by going to Settings → Configure amaroK, and click the Scrobbler icon. You must create an account at the web site in advance. Then, on your amaroK playback window, click on the small boxlike icon at the bottom that has the tooltip "Append Suggestions on." This allows amaroK to add the Audioscrobbler recommendations to your playlist.

But the fun doesn't stop there. amaroK also has an automatic lyric lookup feature. While playing a song, click on the Lyric tab (you must be in the Context view for this to be visible) to download the lyrics. Not every song is in the online database, so be sure to take the time to add lyrics for the ones you do know the words to.

The final feature that won me over to amaroK is its rule-based playlist creation ability. With this feature, you can tell amaroK to play songs that you've never listened to, or all the Jazz albums recorded from 1970 to 1980, or every song from a particular artist that you haven't listened to at least 20 times. To set this up, click on the Playlist sidebar icon. There are several default lists, but we're interested in the ability to create new ones. Click Create Smart-Playlist to open a window where you can specify your list criteria. This is just like creating a filter for email, except that you are applying it to your music collection. Give the playlist a name, specify the criteria (add additional criteria by clicking the plus icon), and save. To play the list, just drag it to the playlist window. amaroK will automatically apply the criteria and present the songs that match.

amaroK has a lot more features (such as the ability to send a playlist to a CD burning program and play Internet radio streams), and it is definitely a player that you should check out—even if KDE is not your preferred desktop.

RhythmBox

http://www.gnome.org/projects/rhythmbox/

RhythmBox is an iTunes work-alike for GNOME. At least, that's what I've heard. I haven't used iTunes for more than five minutes, so I can't compare.

What I can tell you is that RhythmBox is a refreshing and easy-to-use music manager application. Though it lacks the flexibility of amaroK, it makes up for it with a simple interface that is a breeze to figure out and set up so that you can remember where everything is. I like how easy it is to filter your playlist down to a particular artist or album. In fact, in its basic mode, RhythmBox seems to encourage album listening, as opposed to random songs, because there is no obvious playlist window to drag individual songs to.

However, it turns out that the playlist window is the side frame labeled Source. The Help instructions tell you to just drag and drop a song to this frame and you'll be presented with a dialog to name your new playlist (you can then start dragging more songs to it). I found that this didn't work in the versions I installed. Instead, I had to create the playlist manually by going to Music → Playlist → New Playlist (or pressing Ctrl-N).

Though the playlist name is a small target to drop files on, what is great about this method is that it forces you to create a named and saved playlist. Lazy people can quickly build a group of playlists they can reuse later. Unfortunately, it also means that lazy people will soon have a cluttered Source frame with obsolete playlists.

RhythmBox can also play Internet radio streams. There are a few preset stations, but you can add new ones by selecting Music → New Internet Radio Station. You need to know the URL for the broadcast.

CD and DVD Burning

When I first came to Linux, CD burners were fairly rare, recordable CDs cost a dollar or more, and the only burning applications on Linux were run from the command line. Nowadays, everyone has a CD or DVD burner, the media is worth less than a penny, and though Linux users can still burn CDs from the console using commands several lines long, there are also a couple of good GUI burning tools that make the task a bit easier. Don't be fooled, though: these easy-to-use programs are really just pretty interfaces for those same old command-line programs.

Gnomebaker

http://gnomebaker.sourceforge.net

This relatively new application attempts to be to GNOME what K3b (described next) is to KDE users.

There aren't a lot of features to this program. It performs the simple task of burning data and audio CDs or making copies of CDs. At this time, there isn't even support for multi-session CDs, but it is planned for the future. This program is certainly one to keep an eye on.

K3b

http://www.k3b.org

Right now, the almost-unanimous favorite for CD burning under Linux is K3b. This handy program brings CD burning under Linux up to par with what is found on other operating systems. The requirements page at the projects site is worth visiting because many features of K3b aren't enabled until you install the necessary support programs.

You can use K3b to burn data and audio CDs, make copies of CDs, burn video CDs and DVDs, create and burn ISO files, and even rip a DVD and encode it in another format so you can fit it on a smaller disk. All of these features are fully explained in the help file.

I particularly like the way K3b integrates into the KDE desktop. You can right-click on an ISO image or one or more files in Konqueror and choose to burn the selection in K3b, and amaroK allows you to burn a playlist full of songs in K3b with just a click.

K3b makes good use of your hardware, so you won't have a 52x burner running at 8x. Personally, I've never burned a coaster with K3b, despite multitasking on the machine during a burn. As recently as last year, I had trouble setting up permissions to be able to burn from a non-root account, but with recent distributions, that problem appears to have corrected itself.

Digital Images

With the advent of cheap digital cameras and camera phones, you probably find that you have more digital images than you know how to handle. Linux has several excellent programs for editing your digital images and managing the results.

The GIMP

http://www.gimp.org

The GNU Image Manipulation Program (GIMP) is the premier image-editing program for Linux. It is a large, complex program that deserves a book of its own. There are also ports that you can run under Windows and Mac OS X.

Though the GIMP is often compared to Adobe Photoshop, most professional graphic artists claim that it falls quite short of being a replacement for that commercial program. Still, many will also readily agree that the GIMP is more than sufficient for hobbyists.

There are plenty of web tutorials that teach you how to perform various touch-up tasks with the GIMP. It is a complex program with a lot of flexibility. If you just want to give it a quick spin, open an image in it and play around with the various Filters and Script-Fu effects.

digiKam

http://www.digikam.org

You can use digiKam to manage your collection of digital images, as well as to perform light image editing. It is a KDE application, but it's not part of the core project.

digiKam can interface directly with many digital cameras and download the images into its albums. You can also import images directly from the disk or from another attached storage device. From there, you can organize your photos, tag them with metadata for easier searches and organization, or perform light touch-ups like image rotation and red-eye removal. The editing abilities can be expanded through plug-ins, so be on the lookout for new ones that may add features you desire.

digiKam enables you to add metadata to your image to make it easier to search for in the future. The tag editing window allows you to move forward and back in a collection of images, making it easier to add tagging data without a lot of right-clicking and menu selecting. In addition, with just a few clicks, you can assign multiple tags to an image, making short work of the tagging process.

All in all, this is a great program for managing your photo collection.

F-Spot

http://www.gnome.org/projects/f-spot/

F-Spot is a new image-editing program that integrates nicely into the GNOME environment. It has several features that make it easy to use for large image collections or for people who make use of the Flickr web site.

I'll admit, I haven't bitten hard on the whole digital camera craze (I also don't have a cell phone). But spending just 10 minutes with this program had me itching to dig out the camera and start snapping some pictures. What sold me was the date-based way the program handled my images and the ease of tagging. It almost made it fun.

The date browsing feature is accessed with a simple chronological toolbar along the top of the main window. Bars on the graph indicate pictures taken on that date. The higher the bar, the more images. Browsing images this way made it very easy to identify all the images that I took last year during a trip to Oregon, as well as the pictures that were centered around Christmas. When you click on a date in the toolbar, the thumbnail view takes you to the pictures on that date, and the first image "throbs" for a second—just to get your attention.

Tagging is super easy. In the frame on the left, you can right-click and create new tags and new categories, which hold collections of tags. After creating tags for pictures of my wife and myself—as well as tags for Oregon, Portland, and Mt. Hood—I began the process of tagging the images. It was quite simple. Holding down the Control key, I clicked on each image that belonged to a particular tag, then right-clicked on the last one, and selected the appropriate tag. In a matter of about 5 minutes, I had assigned about 200 photographs to multiple categories. I never had so much fun performing an annoying chore.

F-Spot also has a limited set of image-editing features. These are not as extensive as those in digiKam, but they will no doubt improve in the future. You can also easily export your images to the web photo repository Flickr (*http://flickr.com*), while retaining your tags and categories, if you choose. digiKam should be gaining this feature shortly in the form of a plug-in.

Games

Though everyone buys computers to do homework, keep track of personal finances, and prepare the occasional presentation for work—what computers really get used for are surfing the Internet and playing games. I've already shown you what a good OS Linux is for Internet fun, but is it any good at the first-person-shooter kind of fun?

The answer is a definite maybe. Yes, the Linux operating system is perfectly capable of playing highly advanced games with lifelike graphics and 5.1 digital surround sound. There are no real *technical* barriers to Linux being used as an outstanding gaming platform.

The barriers are purely market-driven. There simply are not enough Linux users to justify a game company porting or designing a game to run natively on Linux. However, there are a few exceptions to this rule, as there are native ports of Doom 3, Neverwinter Nights, Unreal Tournament 2004, America's Army, and older games such as Civilization: Call to Power, Tribes 2, Heroes of Might and Magic III, and other, less popular games. The point is that games that run natively on the Linux OS are few and far between, and there aren't nearly enough to satisfy the typical gamer.

However, if you really want to run commercial games on Linux, you should look a the Cedega software from Transgaming (*http://www.transgaming.com*), which is a translation layer between the Windows game and the Linux OS that allows you to run many popular game at near-native speeds. The software isn't free, but at a subscription price of $5 per month, it isn't bad. The software also isn't perfect, so do research at the Cedega web site to ensure games will play.

Commercial games aren't the only ones that are fun to play. Many classic arcade and console games are supported using a technology called Xmame. This program emulates the hardware environments that these games originally ran in, enabling you to play classic PacMan just as it was in the arcade when you were young. Visit the Xmame web page at *http://x.mame.net* for more information.

Linux is also a good platform for playing Java- and Flash-based online games, which are particularly popular with children. For some games, the speed is a little slow, and for others, the sound may not work, but usually your experience will be comparable to what you can obtain in Windows.

Finally, there are a lot of open source games you can play, from airplane simulators, to tank battles, to card games. Speaking of which: if you like solitaire, you should try the pysol package available from *http://www.pysol.org*—it contains more than 300 variants of solitaire!

There are several online Linux gaming resources you can turn to for more information:

> *http://happypenguin.org*
> *http://icculus.org*
> *http://www.linuxgames.com*
> *http://freshmeat.net*

When visiting this last web site, you should click on Browse and then on the Games/Entertainment subcategory. You'll find more than 2,000 open source games listed there.

## CHAPTER 6

Add, Remove, and Update Programs

On Linux, the tasks of adding, removing, and updating programs are collectively known as *package management*. Many people regard this as one of the most difficult tasks to perform in Linux. Though installing programs is not always easy, the problem most new users face is not understanding that Linux handles program installs very differently than Windows.

For example, with Linux, you will seldom download a single install file from a web site, double-click it, answer a few questions in a wizard, and then have an installed program complete with an icon in your KDE or GNOME menu. Instead, it is more common to launch your distribution's package management tool, search for the program you want to install, select it, and let the package program install it for you.

It is debatable as to which method is better, but I can tell you one thing: with most Linux distributions, you can refresh not only your operating system, but all of your installed programs with just one or two commands. All the security updates, all of the bug fixes, and all of the new features are available to you in an instant—for all of your programs. Think about that for a moment.

Most package managers connect over the Internet to a set of repositories that list all of the programs available for that distribution. Though each distribution comes with its own set of repositories, you might want to add a few third party ones to extend the amount of software you can install, or because you've found a repository that is more up-to-date than the default. Most additional repositories are maintained by enthusiasts of the distribution but are still safe to use. Quite often you have to turn to a third-party repository to find packages that enable various forms of multimedia playback, such as playing DVDs.

This chapter will show you the basics of using each of the preferred package managers of each distribution. This includes adding new repositories; updating your local list of software; adding, removing, and updating software; and querying your package manager to find out which programs are available and what they are called. I wrap up this chapter by telling you how to install one-off RPM packages and the basics of compiling and installing a program from source code.

Fedora

Fedora is an RPM-based distribution. The package management tools for Fedora are in a state of flux. You will find the legacy holdover, up2date, from Fedora's Red Hat days as well as the current default, Yum (Yellow Dog Updater Modified). Some Fedora users find apt-rpm better suits their needs, and they configure their system to run that instead of Yum.

This section will focus upon Yum, which was chosen over apt-rpm by the Fedora maintainers because it provided one-stop-shopping package management for a distribution that would run on multiple processor types—something apt-rpm couldn't do at the time.

Yum is a command-line tool and fairly simple to use. What follows is a list of commands that you can use for the basic functions of installing, upgrading, and removing packages. You must have an active Internet connection for Yum to work—even if you're just searching through the packages.

Yum doesn't sync with a remote repository; instead, it queries the repository directly each time you run a command.

yum install *packagename1 [packagename2...]*

Use this command to install a program. It requires you to know the exact name of the package and allows you to enter more than one package name if you want to install multiple packages with one command.

yum check-update

This command performs a check against all of your Yum repositories and tells you which of your installed programs have updates available.

yum update *packagename1 [packagename2...]*

This command will update the specified package, if an update is available.

yum update

With this command, you can upgrade all of the software in your system with the latest available packages. This approach is far superior to using Microsoft's Windows Update site, which upgrades only the OS; this command can potentially upgrade every piece of software on your system.

yum remove *packagename1 [packagename2...]*

Use this command to remove a program from your computer.

yum search *criteria*

Use this command to search your repositories to find packages that match your criteria, then pick the correct one to install. This search may take some time. An example criteria is searching for the term dvd in order to find any DVD players or libraries.

yum list available

Lists all of the packages available through your Yum repositories.

Yum comes configured with a set of default repositories, either in the *etc/yum.conf* file or as several files in *etc/yum.repos.d/*. From time to time, you might need to add additional repositories in order to install the programs you want. Here are a few resources that you'll want to add right away or use to find repositories where specific packages are stored. Each site posts the necessary information for adding the repository to your configuration. Be warned that some repositories do not play well with others, which means you may end up with packages installed multiple times, programs that won't run, and possibly a borked system. Read the information available at each site before using it.

http://rpm.livna.org
> This site contains additional software that could not be included in Fedora Core for licensing reasons. A lot of multimedia packages can be found here. Visit the Configuration page to learn how to add this repository to your system. This repository is an add-on to your standard ones; it does not replace them.

http://freshrpms.net
> A collection of packages maintained by Matthias Saou. This resource complements the standard Fedora repositories. Read the list of maintained packages to find out whether there is any reason for you to add this to your repositories. To configure this repository, visit *http://ayo.freshrpms.net*, click on the appropriate "Downloads for yum" link, and install the *noarch.rpm* file you'll find there (the command is **rpm -ivh *packagename***).

http://www.fedoratracker.org
> You can use this site to find repositories containing programs you want to install that aren't found in the official repositories. If you search by repository, the site will even provide the configuration lines necessary to add to your *etc/yum.conf* file so you can pull down the packages right away. Sadly, this site has not yet been updated for Fedora Core 4, but hopefully it will be soon.

http://rpm.pbone.net

> This site helps you find packages or determine which files are in a package, which is particularly useful when you're trying to track down a dependency and don't know which package it is in. You can also search for SUSE and Mandriva RPMs here.

http://dag.wieers.com/home-made/apt/

> A fairly exhaustive site that maintains extra packages or updates to core packages.

FreshRPMs, Dag, and other sites are combining their efforts to create a definitive alternative RPM source to be found at *http://rpmforge.net*. This site is still under construction but is certainly a place to keep an eye on for future developments.

If you prefer to use a GUI for package management, you should tryout the two available for Yum, available with these commands:

```
# yum install yumex
# yum install kyum
```

Gentoo

Gentoo's package management solution, known as *portage*, is one of the features that sets it apart from other distributions. Like Ubuntu's apt-get, it automatically handles package dependencies, which makes it very easy to install practically any program with a single command. Unlike Ubuntu, Gentoo does not install precompiled binaries; instead, it downloads the source code for the program and its dependencies, and then compiles them based upon the compile-time options you pass to it. Though you can enter these options when you install a program, Gentoo also has a centralized configuration file (*/etc/make.conf*) where you can enter a set of defaults to use with most programs. Visit the Gentoo documentation web site (*http://www.gentoo.org/doc/en/index.xml*) to learn more about portage.

The following commands and descriptions should be enough to get you started using portage. All of these commands should be run as root. Many of these commands accept options that are covered in Table 6-1.

emerge *packagename1* *[packagename2...]*

Use this command to install one or more programs. You need to know the exact program name. This command is frequently combined with the p, a, and v options.

emerge sync

This command synchronizes your local list of packages with those available on the Gentoo server. This is necessary so portage knows which programs are available.

emerge -u *packagename1* *[packagename2...]*

Adding the –u option tells emerge to upgrade the programs listed. This command is frequently combined with the D and a options.

emerge -u system

This command updates all of the Gentoo system files— those that are core to the operating of the OS. You can combine this with the D and a options.

emerge -u world

This command updates all of the programs you installed on the system to the latest version available. Frequently combined with D and a options.

emerge unmerge *packagename1* *[packagename2...]*

Use this command to remove a package from the system.

emerge -s *criteria*

This command searches the title of the package to find ones that match your criteria. If you add the --searchdescr option (–S) you can match against the package description. The criteria can be entered as a regular expression. Searches can take a long time to perform, particularly when you are searching the description.

Table 6-1. emerge command options

emerge option	Action
−a	Prompts you for a Yes or No after portage determines which packages need to be installed. Faster than running emerge with a −p.
−u	Updates packages and their immediate dependencies to the best version available.
−D	Forces portage to do a deep scan of dependencies, including dependencies of dependencies, and to recompile those. Particularly useful after you've upgraded GCC.
−v	Runs emerge with verbose output so you can see which USE flags affect a package.
−p	Pretends to emerge. Used to see which packages would be installed.
−f	Fetches only the required source files; does not compile and install the programs.
−l	One-shot install. Using this option doesn't add the package to the world database, so it won't be updated automatically in the future. Useful for large packages like KDE or X that you may want to update less frequently.
−s	Searches the package name for a match to the criteria you specify.
−S	Searches the package name and description for a match to the criteria you specify.

Because all programs are compiled, it can take quite a bit of time to install large programs; KDE, for example can take between 12 and 60 hours, depending upon the speed of your machine. Because of this, you'll want to set emerge to allow other programs their fair use of the processor. This is called *nicing* the process, and you can do it two ways. From the command line, you can run an emerge command like this:

```
# nice -n19 emerge mozilla-firefox
```

If you don't specify an n value, then the command usually defaults to 10. The higher the number, the nicer it runs emerge, with 19 being the highest. Negative numbers are "not nice" and tend to hog CPU time.

Alternatively, you can set the niceness value in */etc/make.conf*. Open this file in a text editor, scroll to the bottom, and add this option:

```
PORTAGE_NICENESS = 19
```

Doing this will always run emerge at the nicest level possible.

Gentoo has the concept of a stable and unstable branch (known as the *arch branch* in Gentoo). Sometimes the version of a package that you want to install is in the arch branch. To force portage to allow you to install the package you want, you must add the package to the */etc/portage/package.keyword* file. For example, if Version 1.1 of Firefox is marked unstable (~x86 arch), but you want to install it, you would add the following line to your *package.keyword* file (first create the file if it doesn't exist):

```
>www-client/mozilla-firefox-bin-1.0.3 ~x86
```

As you can see, you can use an operand to specify that you want to use any version of mozilla-firefox that is greater than 1.0.3. The ~x86 entry represents the desire to use the arch branch of the x86 processor architecture. Other architecture's have their own arch branch. It is fairly common for users to install packages from arch.

For more information about portage, read the manpages for portage, emerge, ebuild, and make.conf.

Mandriva

Another RPM-based distribution, Mandriva favors its internally developed package management program *urpmi*. This is the first RPM-based package management tool to have dependency checking. But the tool is showing its age and many Mandrake users now prefer apt-rpm tools, such as the one also used by Fedora users. With the recent purchase of Connectiva, the developer of apt-rpm, you can expect apt-rpm to receive increased attention in the future.

In addition to the command-line tool urpmi, Mandriva has a GUI tool for package management. I'll introduce you to both.

To use urpmi, you must log in as root at the command line. The following list provides you with the commands you need to perform basic functions, such as installing, upgrading, removing, and searching:

urpmi *packagename1* [*packagename2*...]

> This command is doubly useful. Not only does it install one or more packages when you specify their names, it also displays possible packages if it can't resolve a package name to a single file. It's like an install and search combined.

urpmi.update -a

> Use this command to sync your local list of files with your configured repositories. This command should be run before upgrading or installing new packages.

urpmi --update *packagename1* [*packagename2*...]

> This command will update the specified packages if there are newer versions available. Mandriva requires you to add special update sites for this to work (how to do this is covered later in this section).

urpmi --auto-select

> This command will upgrade everything on your system if there is a newer version available; however, it will not upgrade your kernel.

urpme *packagename1* [*packagename2*...]

> Use this command to remove one or more packages. If urpme (note that this command ends with an e) can't resolve the package name, it will present a list with ones that come closest.

urpmf *criteria*

Since regular urpmi performs searches for you, there is no need for a separate command. This one, however, will let you search for a package that contains a given file: useful for when you are told that you need to install a library but don't know which package contains it. If you preface your criteria with **lib/**criteria or **bin/**criteria, this command will search only for libraries or program binaries, respectively.

urpmi is fairly flexible in how it handles its repositories, which it calls "sources." It counts the original install CDs as one set of sources (and seems to ask for them constantly), but you can also configure it to use other removable media or remote filesystems as a source. For example, in order to get updates to Mandriva, you must configure it to use an update source, as Mandriva does not update the files in the core source.

The easiest way to add new sources is by visiting the web site *http://easyurpmi.zarb.org*. At this web site, you must specify exactly which version of Mandriva you are using and your processor type (the architecture). This is important. If you're uncertain, run the following command:

```
$ cat /etc/mandrake-release
Mandrakelinux release 10.2 (Limited Edition 2005) for i586
```

Armed with this knowledge, you can choose the appropriate options in step 1, then click the button to proceed to step 2 (it's actually important that you click—don't just scroll down). Here you can select which sources you want to add. There are essentially four types:

Main

These are the same packages that came on your install CDs, so you really don't have to add them. Still, you might consider adding one and then removing your CDs as sources. Doing this saves you from having to fetch your CDs to install a new package.

Updates

If you want to receive official updates to your installed programs, you need to add one of these mirrors. Even if your system is already configured for this, you might consider finding a faster mirror and adding it.

Contrib

These are community-created and -contributed packages. There are a lot of useful things here, and you certainly should consider adding these packages.

PLF

The PLF sources stand for Penguin Liberation Front; they contain packages that Mandrake hasn't included with the CDs for various licensing reasons, such as encrypted DVD playback support. If you add the PLF sources, you should also add Contrib as some PLF packages depend upon it. The –free source includes only software that meets the Free Software Foundation definition of "free." The –non–free source includes useful software that isn't officially free. Note that this doesn't mean it is illegal—just that it isn't under a Free license.

Once you've selected the sources to add, click "Proceed to next step (3)." This step creates the command that you need to enter as root to add the sources you selected. Simply copy and paste these lines, one at a time, into a root terminal, and press Enter. That's it.

Removing a package source is fairly easy. The *urpmi. removemedia* command does all the work for you. Run it once without any arguments to see what sources are installed. Then run it again with the name of the source, or part of the name, and the utility will attempt to find matches. For example, this command will remove all of your Installation CD sources (run as root):

```
# urpmi.removemedia Installation
```

If you run the command with just the –a option, you'll remove all your media sources at once, which is a handy way of starting fresh and is something you might do before adding the sources at *http://easyurpmi.zarb.org*.

After seeing how powerful and easy urpmi is, I don't know why you'd want to use a GUI package manger, but if you do, you can launch it by clicking K Menu → System → Configuration → Configure Your Computer. This launches the MandrakeLinux Control Center, and it just so happens that the default selection is Software Management. The following list contains descriptions of how to perform the tasks already discussed in the urpmi section.

TIP

The same programs are installed under the Configuration → Packaging menu, but this is a more convenient way to use the programs.

Install

Click the icon for "Look at installable software and install software packages." When the screen comes up, you can perform a search for your packages by name or description and check the box to indicate you want to install it. You are then presented with a dialog telling you which dependencies will also be installed; click OK to approve. Click the Install button in the lower left to run the installation.

Synchronize with your repositories

This happens automatically each time you launch the tool. It's a bit annoying, as slow mirrors can suck up a lot of time and a full sync isn't always necessary.

Upgrade all installed programs and add new dependencies

Click "Look at available updates and apply any fixes or updates to installed packages" and, when prompted, click Yes to the request to sync. When this is done, the

---

window will display which packages are available for update. Just check the ones you want to update and click Install. It is a good idea to check for updates after you install new programs from the Main source.

Remove a program

Click "Look at installed software and uninstall software packages" and, when prompted, click Yes to continue. In the window that comes up, search for the packages you want to remove, agree when Mandriva tells you which dependencies need to be removed, and then click the Remove button. Pay attention to the dependencies being removed: Mandriva is not very conservative in its removal policies, and you might find that you need to add a package again.

Search for a program

Each mini-utility includes its own search functions.

SUSE

SUSE is an RPM-based distribution like Fedora. Most package management is done through the SUSE configuration tool YaST. You typically cannot use RPMs created for other distributions, and I suggest that you don't even try unless you really know what you are doing.

To launch YaST in KDE, click K Menu → System → YaST; in GNOME, click Desktop → YaST. You'll need to supply your root password, as YaST requires superuser privileges to perform software installs.

Here are descriptions of the basic tasks you'll want to perform with YaST:

Install

Click once on the "Install and Remove Software" icon. A new window will open in which you can search for the package you want to install. Once you locate it, check the box next to the name, and click Accept at the bottom of the window. You might be prompted for the SUSE CD/DVD to complete the install if you haven't set up the SUSE FTP repository (I describe how to do that in just a bit).

Synchronize with your repositories

Click on "Change Source of Installation." In the new window, click on the source you want to update, click Edit, and choose Refresh. This may take some time with slow online sources.

Upgrade all installed programs and install security updates

Click Online Update to run the YaST module to update all of your software. This process loads a screen where you can select an installation source (pick one geographically near you), and then click Next. YaST will determine which new updates are available and present you with a list. Security updates are selected automatically, and you can select additional packages to install. When you are finished making selections, click Accept.

Remove a program

This is the same as installing a program, except that this time you need to click in the box next to the program name until a trash icon appears. Then click Accept at the bottom of the window.

Search for a program

The install and remove package program has its own search built in.

As you can see, YaST is very easy to use. Technically speaking, the GUI program is called YaST2, and the command-line version, which I haven't discussed, is called YaST. The reason I'm not going to cover the command-line version is that it doesn't perform dependency checking, which makes it fairly useless for installing large numbers of programs. If you do need to install one-off programs that aren't in the SUSE repositories, then use command-line RPM instead, which I describe in the section "Using RPMs," later in this chapter.

There are a few SUSE repositories you might be interested in. Adding them to your sources is quite simple. Inside YaST, click "Change Source of Installation." In the window that comes up, you can add additional media sources (repositories). The sources you add will be used by the "Install and Remove Software" program. I'll walk you through the process of adding the SUSE FTP site, so you won't need to have the CDs or DVDs always with you (though you will need Internet access):

1. Click Add and choose FTP. (Not all mirror sites are FTP, so be sure to choose the protocol that matches the site you are connecting to.)

2. Enter **ftp.suse.com** server name. Preferably, use a mirror from the list found at *http://www.novell.com/products/ linuxprofessional/downloads/ftp/int_mirrors.html*. To use the mirror at Corvalis, Oregon, for example, enter the server name *ftp.oregonstate.edu*. It's good to use a mirror because it is often faster than the main site. If you chose a slow mirror accidentally, pick another.

3. In the field "Directory on Server," enter the path to the architecture and version of SUSE you are using. For example, to add the SUSE 9.3 directory for i386 computers, enter the path **/pub/suse/suse/i386/9.3**. This path is specific to each server, and you might need to browse the site to figure out what it is. As you can see, the Oregon State site has two levels of *suse/* directories.

4. Most web sites are anonymous, so just click OK at this point. YaST will update its list of packages with what is on the server and then return you to the main window.

5. Disable any repositories you don't want to use by clicking on their name and then clicking "Enable or Disable."

Other than the repositories that duplicate what you already have on the install media, there are a few you might want to add, as they give you better multimedia support or more up-to-date software. This Wiki page lists several alternative repositories: *http://www.susewiki.org/index.php?title=Finding_RPMs*. The YaST sources can be added in the manner just described. The other sites can be used to download individual RPMs. Perhaps the most useful to desktop users is the Packman YaST source, which has a lot of updated and non-crippled (able to play DVDs, for example) multimedia programs. I highly recommend adding Packman.

Let's pretend you've added the KDE sources from the Wiki and want to update everything from that source to the latest version. Here's how to do it:

1. Click "Install and Remove Software."
2. The window may take some time to come up as the program checks the sources. When it does come up, YaST should have automatically selected which programs are available to be updated based upon the versions in the repositories you just added.
3. Click Accept to start the update process.

The list of packages can be a little confusing because the programs with regular checks next to them are merely placeholders for programs already installed. After all, at this moment, YaST doesn't know whether you intend to add, update, or remove programs. The ones that are really being updated have a strange green, white, and black Z symbol.

Ubuntu

Ubuntu is a new distribution based upon the venerable Debian distro. In the year since its release, it has earned many fans, a lot of press, and is starting to be regarded as one of the best Linux desktop distributions available. Ubuntu is a lot like—but not exactly like—a Debian system.

If you are a Debian user, you will feel right at home updating and maintaining an Ubuntu system, but if you are new to Linux or Debian, this short section will tell you everything you essentially need to know to handle package management.

Like Debian, Ubuntu uses the apt system for package management. You can run several easy-to-remember commands at the command line, or you can make use of the preconfigured GUI tool, Synaptic. I'll walk you through both.

The following list describes the commands necessary for installing, updating, removing, and searching packages. You must be root to run these commands.

apt-get install *packagename1* *[packagename2...]*
> With this command and the correct name of a package, you can install a new program and all its dependencies. The command will take more than one package name.

apt-get update
> This command synchronizes your local cache of available programs with those listed in your repository. You should run this command before installing new packages to make sure you are getting the latest ones available.

apt-get upgrade
> Run this command to upgrade all your installed packages to the latest versions available. This command will not remove existing packages or install new packages.

apt-get dist-upgrade
> This command is probably the best way to upgrade all your programs to the latest versions because it has additional dependency and conflict-resolution abilities. These enable your upgrade to not only update installed programs, but add new programs if they are necessary to meet dependencies.

apt-get remove *packagename1 [packagename2...]*

This command works just like install, except that it removes programs instead.

apt-cache search *criteria*

This command searches your local cache list of programs to find ones that match your criteria. You can use regular expressions in your criteria; the search is performed against both the title and description of the package. From here, you should be able to find the one you want to install.

apt-cache show *packagename*

After you've searched for and found a package, you can use this command to display more information about it.

dpkg -i *packagename*

Use this command to install a single Debian package file (*.deb*) that is not part of a repository.

Synaptic just performs the same functions you see here, but because it is graphical, new users may feel more comfortable with it. To launch it, click System → Administration → Synaptic Package Manager. You'll then need to provide your password to load the program. Usage is fairly simple. The following list mirrors the previous one, but it tells you how to perform these functions using the GUI:

Install

To install a program, check the box next to program name in the listing and choose "Mark for Installation." This option may then display a window showing you which additional packages need to be installed to support your chosen program (the dependencies). Click Mark on this window, then click Apply on the main toolbar. Yet another window is displayed; here you can review what will be installed before you click Apply to actually run the installation.

Synchronize with your repositories
　　Click the Reload button on the main toolbar.

Upgrade all installed programs
　　After syncing, click Mark All Upgrades on the main tool-
　　bar. In the window that appears, click Default Upgrade.
　　Then click the Apply button on the main toolbar, review
　　the programs to be installed, and click Apply in that
　　window.

Upgrade all installed programs and add new dependencies
　　Identical to the previous steps, except that you click
　　Smart Upgrade instead of Default.

Remove a program
　　Just like install: find the program you want to remove,
　　click the box, and in the menu that appears, choose one
　　of the removal options. The only difference between
　　these two is that the complete removal deletes configura-
　　tion files as well.

Search for a program
　　Click the Search button and enter your criteria. Use the
　　drop-down list to specify which information fields will be
　　searched. A Description and Name search will take
　　longer than just a Name, but has a greater chance of
　　returning useful hits.

From time to time, you'll find you need to add additional
repositories to install programs not provided by the Ubuntu
maintainers. This is particularly true of "non-free" programs—those that don't meet Ubuntu's definition of free
software. Java and many multimedia codecs fall into this category. You can add a repository through Synaptic or by editing the */etc/apt/sources.list* directly. Two repositories that
you'll want to enable right away are Universe and Multiverse. Instructions follow for how to do that using both the
command-line and GUI methods.

To enable Universe, open */etc/apt/sources.list* in your preferred text editor and locate these lines:

```
# deb http://us.archive.ubuntu.com/ubuntu hoary universe
# deb-src http://us.archive.ubuntu.com/ubuntu hoary
universe
```

Uncomment these lines by removing the # signs, save the file, and then run **apt-get update** to sync with the repository.

To enable Multiverse, open your */etc/apt/sources.list* file again, scroll to the bottom, and add these lines:

```
deb http://archive.ubuntu.com/ubuntu hoary multiverse
deb-src http://archive.ubuntu.com/ubuntu hoary multiverse
```

Save your changes, exit, and then run **apt-get update** to sync with the Multiverse repository.

WARNING

Universe and Multiverse are not officially supported and are considered "use at your own risk." That said, most everyone does take the risk.

With the GUI, it is only slightly harder. Launch Synaptic, then go to Settings → Repositories. In the dialog that appears, click the Add button. In this small window, check the Universe and Multiverse boxes, then close out of the windows by clicking OK. Synaptic will report that the repositories have changed and ask if you want to sync, which you probably do. (There appears to be a bug in this little update program that prevents the dialog box from remembering that you added Universe and Multiverse.)

To add a completely custom repository, you'll need what is known as the APT line, which any repository you encounter should give you. You can either just drop this into your *sources.list* file yourself, or add it through the GUI. The process is the same, except that instead of selecting a repository

---

from the list, you should click Custom and add the APT line to the dialog that appears.

Using RPMs

Fedora, Mandriva, and SUSE are all RPM-based distributions. Though they each have vast package repositories, from time to time, you might still need to install RPM packages that aren't available through those official channels. This is often the case when you want to update to the latest version of a program, such as Firefox, and the distro repositories haven't yet picked up the latest version.

The solution is to find an RPM for the program and install it manually. This is not difficult in the least: just remember to get an RPM for your distribution and preferably for the same version of your distro. A Fedora RPM is not really designed to install and run on a SUSE system, and you risk complications by trying.

The only real problem with this method is that it does not download needed dependencies for you. This problem might require you to manually track down and install several packages, commonly referred to as *dependency hell*: the avoidance of this state is one of the several reasons package managers were created in the first place.

Once you've downloaded an RPM, you have a couple of choices for how to install it. Inside your desktop environment, you can probably just click on the file to open it. Your distribution will propose a program that can handle this, you agree, and the package gets installed. After that, it is pretty much just a matter of following the prompts or using the package manager as I described earlier.

To install an RPM from the command line, just use the following command:

```
$ sudo rpm -ivh packaname.rpm
```

The switches are fairly simple: –i for install, –v for verbose, and –h to show a progress bar. A failed dependency error looks like this:

```
error: Failed dependencies:
  libcrypto.so.5 is needed by
    sylpheed-claws-1.9.12-1.2.fc4.i386
  libssl.so.5 is needed by
    sylpheed-claws-1.9.12-1.2.fc4.i386
```

With an error like this, you need to track down the *libcrypto. so.5* and *libssl.so.5* libraries. Use your package manager's search ability to find these files, install them, and then try the previous rpm command again.

A successful install looks like this:

```
$ sudo rpm -ivh packagename.rpm
Preparing...   ################### [100%]
1:packagename  ################### [100%]
```

To remove a package, replace –i with –e, for erase. There are a lot of other options available for the rpm command; the manpage is your best bet for the complete information.

Build Your Own

If you stick with the programs offered by your package manager, you'll generally find installing software to be a breeze. But if you like the bleeding edge, and want to try out development versions of software or programs that aren't yet available in your package manager, you'll find yourself needing to install packages from source. For those who don't program, this may seem like a daunting idea at first, but it can actually be quite simple—at least, when things go right.

Compiling source code requires that you have the necessary tools installed. Gentoo users will have these automatically, as it is part of the process of setting up a Gentoo system. If you use another distribution, you will probably have to install these programs yourself. Use your package manager to identify the software group for development, and install the recommended packages. In most distributions, this can be done by using the package manager to install *gcc* and its dependencies.

To install a package from source, you generally have to visit its web site to find the archive file with all of the source code. Download this to a directory on your machine; many people like to place downloaded source in a single location, such as */usr/local/src/*. Most source code is packed in a *gzip* or *bzip2* compressed tar archive. *tar* keeps the source files bound together in a single file, and *gzip* and *bzip2* compress this file so that it takes less time to download. Either of the following two commands is usually sufficient to not only decompress the archive but also expand the *tar* file and place all the contained files into their own directory:

```
$ tar -xvzf foo.tar.gz
$ tar -xvjf foo.tar.bz2
```

The first command will expand and untar a *gzip* archive, and the second will do the same for *bzip2*. The difference between the two commands is the −z switch in the first one and the −j in the second. Respectively, these call the *gunzip* or *bunzip2* decompression programs to expand the archive before *tar* opens the tarball (the tar archive).

After you expand the files, change into the newly created directory. Inside, you'll usually find a *README* file that tells you a bit about the software and provides specific instructions for compiling it. If there is an *INSTALL* file present, read that, too, as it may contain more complete install information. The instructions usually boil down to just three steps:

```
$ ./configure
```
This command checks out your system to make sure everything that is needed for compiling is present. It pulls in any environment variables and settings necessary to make a program that will run on your computer.

```
$ make
```
This command actually builds the software. For large packages, running this might take some time—it really depends upon the speed of your processor.

```
# make install
```
This final step actually installs the compiled code in the proper places. Note that it must be run as root in order to get the software in the proper places.

And that is typically all it takes to install software from source. Perhaps the hardest part is finding out which command you need to run to launch your newly installed program, and adding a launcher to your desktop environment menus.

For some software, you'll find that you can't build the program because you need to have some other program installed or you need that other program's source code. This is the source code variant of dependency hell. When you get the error messages related to these problems, your next step should be to install the needed software. First, check your package manager to see whether you can install it that way. For many distributions, this might mean installing the *packagename-src* package. If your package manager doesn't have the needed program, you'll probably have to download the source, and compile and install it manually. It can take some time to track down everything you need, but don't give up, and take notes. They can help you troubleshoot a problem or come in handy the next time you need to install the program on another machine.

## CHAPTER 7

Configuration

Perhaps the most frustrating aspect of using a computer is having hardware that you can't figure out how to make work. You plug in a new wireless network card and two hours and nine reboots later, you still don't have it working; your new printer looks great sitting on your desktop, but you can't get it to print a single letter, let alone a full-color photograph. I wish I could say that with Linux all of your hardware will "Just Work," as the Mac saying goes, but that simply isn't true. Configuring some types of hardware in Linux can be a challenge.

The situation is far from bleak, though. The Linux kernel is gaining support for new hardware on a daily basis, and hardware vendors are contributing code and specifications to kernel developers at an unprecedented rate. When I first used Linux, I had to send my laptop off to a development company to have an X driver created for it; now configuring my graphics card is usually simpler than getting it to work under Windows. Usually.

And that is why I've written this chapter: to help you through the unusual times. Obviously, I can't be exhaustive in such a small guide, but I believe you'll find the following advice useful in your quest to get your hardware working. At the very least, this information may make it easier for you to find, and understand, the available help online.

Sound

Since the release of the 2.6 kernel and its inclusion of the Advanced Linux Sound Architecture (ALSA) last year, the Linux audio situation is looking remarkably better, but it is still complicated. The ALSA drivers interact with your audio card, audio middle layers interact with the drivers, sometimes a desktop environment audio daemon helps out, and your programs interact with the middle layer. Except, of course, for those programs that aren't configured for ALSA and need to interact with the legacy Open Source Sound (OSS) system, so that you need to add support layer that unites OSS and ALSA. Easy, right?

Well, not always. But maybe this section will help you figure things out. Obviously, you need to follow this advice only if your distribution failed to set up your sound card at all—an increasingly rare occurrence. Here are the steps to getting your sound working:

1. Identify your sound card chip set.
2. Find the ALSA driver that supports your chipset.
3. Load your sound card driver module.
4. Add your user to the audio group so that it has permissions to use the sound device.
5. Unmute and set the volume levels for your sound card.
6. Test.
7. Configure your driver to load at boot. (This step is not necessary if the sound driver is compiled directly into the kernel.)

Here are the details. First off, you need to know something about your sound card, like which chipset it uses. Run the following command to find out a little about your hardware (as root, to be sure that *lspci* is in your path):

```
# lspci | grep -i audio
00:1f.5 Multimedia audio controller:
Intel Corp. 82801DB AC'97 Audio (rev 01)
```

The *lspci* command lists the hardware that the kernel detected on your PCI bus. In the output from this command, I can see that I have an Intel Corp 82801DB chipset.

With this information, I can search the ALSA card support database to find which ALSA driver my card needs. To do this, visit the site *http://www.alsa-project.org/alsa-doc/*, scroll to the bottom of the page, select your manufacturer from the drop-down list, and click Go. This brings you to a page where all the supported chipsets for that manufacturer are listed along with the ALSA driver to use. In my case, I find only one Intel driver, but from the table, it doesn't look like it supports my chipset. Just to be certain, I click on the Details link for the driver anyway, and sure enough, on the next page, it does list my chipset. Looking at the rest of the detail page, I learn that the driver module is specifically called *snd-intel8x0*. (Bookmark this page, as you'll need to refer to it again in just a bit.)

Many Linux kernels are built with all the sound card drivers compiled as modules. If you've built a custom kernel, then you probably already know how to go about adding a specific driver and recompiling. Therefore, the next step is to load the driver with the following command and see what happens:

```
# modprobe snd-intel8x0
#
```

To be certain it is loaded, use this command:

```
# lsmod | grep snd
snd_intel8x0m          19780  1
snd_intel8x0           34240  3
snd_ac97_codec         83704  2
    snd_intel8x0m,snd_intel8x0
```

```
snd_pcm                  96392   5
    snd_intel8x0m,snd_intel8x0,
    snd_ac97_codec,snd_pcm_oss
snd                      58884   13
    snd_intel8x0m,snd_intel8x0,
    snd_ac97_codec,snd_pcm_oss,
    snd_mixer_oss,snd_pcm,snd_timer
snd_page_alloc           10244   3
    snd_intel8x0m,snd_intel8x0,snd_pcm
```

As you can see, a lot more gets loaded to support the single module you added.

Many Linux distributions create an audio group, of which you must be a member to play sounds. Usually, you are automatically a member of this group, but to be sure, run the command **groups** to see which ones your user is a member of. Also, view your /etc/group file to be certain that an audio group even exists (if it doesn't, don't worry about setting audio permissions).

If you do have an audio group and you are not a member, you can use a user management program to add yourself to the group, or you can edit the /etc/group file directly as root and add your name to the appropriate line. The GUI tools are located under the System Preferences menu in GNOME, and in YaST for SUSE. Mandriva provides a tool in its control center, and KDE offers one called KUser that is usually found under K Menu → System.

The next step is to set the volume levels for your card. You can do this with any mixer utility, but it might be simplest to use *alsamixer*, a text-based mixer program that you can use to set your system-wide volume settings. Run it in a terminal as root.

In the text interface, use the left and right arrow keys to move from output to output, the up and down arrows to set the volume, and the M key to toggle mute. The channels you must set are Master and PCM—I usually set mine to 80–90 each—and be sure to unmute. When you're done, press Esc to save.

Now, it's time to test the results. You can load any multimedia program you want and play a music file, but it is probably simpler to try out this command (be sure that your physical speaker volume is turned up):

```
# aplay /usr/share/sounds/alsa/
  Front_Center.wav
Playing WAVE '/usr/share/sounds/alsa/
  Front_Center.wav' : Signed 16 bit
  Little Endian, Rate 48000 Hz, Mono
```

You should hear a voice speaking the words, "Front Center." If you don't have this file, look for another one to play in the */usr/share/sounds* directory.

If everything is working correctly, you now need to configure your system to load the appropriate sound modules on boot. Where this is done varies by distribution—usually */etc/modprobe.conf* for 2.6 series kernels. The lines you add vary depending upon your sound card, but they will look something like this:

```
alias snd-card-0 snd-intel8x0
alias sound-slot-0 snd-intel8x0
```

The details page at the ALSA web site (where you learned which driver to specify for your card) will probably include a configuration file for your card. Just create */etc/modprobe.conf* and paste the suggested text in it.

TIP

The specific instructions you find on the ALSA page for your driver may be a little out of date—they were probably written for a 2.4 series kernel. Try my instructions first, and if they fail, fall back to what is written on the driver page.

You might find that your distribution comes with the program *alsaconf*. If so, you can use this to configure your drivers to load at boot. If you don't have this utility, your distribution may have another method for configuring the sound card. Fedora has a configuration program located at Desktop → System Settings → Soundcard Detection.

Gentoo provides an excellent guide for setting up the sound system; you can view it at *http://www.gentoo.org/doc/en/alsa-guide.xml*. Ubuntu makes use of the Enlightenment Sound Daemon (one of those extra middleware components I mentioned at the beginning of this section), which complicates the situation a little. Look on the Ubuntu forums and Wiki for information about configuring your sound card.

Printing

Printing under Linux used to be a real chore. There were few printer drivers, minimal support for inkjet printers, and the whole print system was based upon the fairly archaic *lpd* program. These days, most Linux distributions make use of the Common Unix Printing System (CUPS), which makes configuring and using printers easier than ever. The technology behind CUPS was good enough for Apple to choose it as the print system for OS X!

Your Linux distribution should come with CUPS already installed and set to run when you boot your machine. All that remains for you to do is set up your printers. Most printers these days are USB, but some still interface with the parallel port. CUPS supports both. There are several ways to set up your printer, depending upon whether you're using GNOME, KDE, or some other desktop environment. I'll walk you through each one. The exact steps may vary for each distribution, but they'll be close enough that you can figure things out.

There are a couple of things to watch out for. For example, a powered-on printer that has just been connected to a SUSE system will probably trigger its auto-hardware detection. At that point, you have the option to run a configuration program (YaST). Do that, and setting up the printer is a breeze.

If, for some reason, the printer setup isn't triggered, you can run the configuration manually by going to the Hardware → Printer module in YaST. If that fails, then try the generic method outlined later in the upcoming "Generic" section.

When it comes time to select your printer driver—if for some reason your printer model doesn't show up in the list—you should try selecting a similar model. For example, if your printer model is 1430, but all you see is 1410 and 1450, select one of those and see if it works.

With some distributions, you might see only a handful of printer models in the selection list. This usually happens when the Foomatic printer drivers are not installed. If you have this problem, it might be solved by installing the *foomatic* package for your distribution and any related Post-script Printer Definition (PPD) packages that define how the printer is controlled. You'll need to stop and restart the CUPS service after the install to make the drivers available.

For the best inkjet drivers, you should install any *gimp-print* packages provided by your distribution, and select that driver when configuring your printer. I've heard that the Epson drivers are particularly good.

GNOME

The tools available for setting up your printer in GNOME vary depending upon your distribution, but they all work similarly. The basic process is to turn on your printer and plug it into your computer. Open the printer configuration program, usually found under Desktop → System Settings or System → Administration. If your printer hasn't already magically appeared, select the option to add a new printer.

This step opens a printer wizard. Tell GNOME how your printer is physically connected to the machine and which printer driver to use. Some of these tools will report any detected printers, but don't be dismayed if yours is not found. Instead, just select the printer type (usually Local) and the printer port (if it's USB and you have no other USB devices, select the first one). If your printer driver doesn't appear, follow the advice given earlier concerning the foomatic and gimp-print packages. Finish the wizard and your printer should appear in the print manager.

KDE

Printers can be configured from the KDE Control Center. The configuration applet is usually under Peripherals, but I've seen it under System Administration as well. By default, this screen is run with your user's permissions. You need to click the Administrator Mode button in order to be allowed to create new printers.

Click Add → Add Printer/Class to start the new printer wizard. Walk through this wizard selecting the connection method, the connecting port (your printer model should show up associated with one of the parallel or USB ports), and the printer make and model. For the rest of the questions, you can accept the defaults until you get to the name screen, where you must give the printer a name. After a few more clicks, you're finished.

Back at the printer configuration screen, you can right-click on your new printer and send a test page, or you can set the printer as the default for the system or user.

The KDE Print Center is pretty useful. From here, you can stop and start your printers, delete print jobs, or move them to other printers. Be sure to explore more of it at some point. You might also be interested in investigating the tools available using the protocol helper print:/ (type that into a Konqueror Location field).

All KDE applications should make use of the printer you've configured, but if you find that other programs, like Mozilla or Adobe Acrobat, are not aware of your printer, simply tell them to use the device *kprinter*. By doing this, whatever printer output the program sends is captured and relayed to KDE. The regular KDE printer dialog will appear, and you can choose which printer to print to at that time. I've usually found it best to choose my printer options, such as how many pages to print, in the first dialog instead of the KDE-specific one.

Generic

CUPS itself provides a web-based interface for adding and managing printers and print queues. You can reach it from your machine by going to *http://localhost:631*. A web page will open up and you'll see several links. The most important at this time is Manage Printer. Click it to be taken to the screen where you can add a new printer.

Adding a printer requires root privileges for CUPS, and your regular root account may not be configured for that yet. If the system root username and password don't get you in, you'll need to make a small adjustment to allow access. Enter this command at a prompt as root:

```
# lppasswd -g sys -a root
Enter Password: ********
Enter Password again: ********
```

The passwords you enter can be whatever you want within the restrictions that the password be at least six characters long and contain at least one letter and number.

With that out of the way, you can now click the Add Printer link, fill in the root username and new password, and begin setting up a printer.

In the first screen, you just need to fill out some descriptive information. Give your printer a name, and, if you want, a location and a description. Then click Continue.

In the next screen, choose the method of connecting to your printer. For local printers, this is almost always USB or parallel port. Hopefully, one of those connections will show that it is aware of your printer; for example, the first USB port might have the printer model in parentheses. If so, select that; if not, select the first port of your connection type, and then click Continue.

On the next couple of screens, you'll first select your printer make and then the specific model. When you're finished making these selections, your new printer will be added and you can print a test page by going to the Printers link.

Each set-up printer has a configuration page. Click the Configure link to go to it. Here you can specify several settings specific to your printer model.

Wired Networking

Wired networking generally just works under Linux. The kernel has support for a very large range of network cards, and most distributions have hardware detection programs that accurately detect the card and load the appropriate module.

Many of the distributions come with a network configuration panel. These work, to a certain extent. For Fedora, the applet is found under Desktop → System Settings → Network; Mandriva has a networking applet in the Mandrake Control Center; SUSE, of course, provides a network program in YaST; and Ubuntu provides a tool under System → Administration → Networking.

Each of these tools can help you configure a network card that has already been detected, which is almost all of them. Some of these tools can even handle wireless network cards; particularly the tools available in Mandriva, SUSE, and Ubuntu. Use these tools to configure your WEP key or specify which network to connect to.

One problem users do encounter from time to time is that when a network cable is disconnected and then plugged back in, the network card doesn't always realize the cable has been inserted, and thus does not retrieve up-to-date information about the network. This happens a lot to laptop users as they roam from home to work and back.

It is possible for Linux to detect the insertion of a network cable in an Ethernet card. I have no idea why all distributions aren't configured to detect this and then configure the network card, but, thankfully, it is relatively easy for you to set up.

First, you need to install the *ifplugd* program using your package management program. This program performs the actual detection of an inserted or removed cable and then uses your distribution's normal interface management tools to configure the card.

After installation, you merely need to tell *ifplugd* which interfaces to monitor and set it to run upon boot. The configuration file is normally in */etc/ifplugd/ifplugd.conf*, */etc/conf.d/ifplugd*, or */etc/default/ifplugd*. Open this file and add the interfaces you want to monitor (eth0, eth1, wlan0, etc.—run *ifconfig* as outlined next if you don't know the name of your interface) to the INTERFACES line. After that, start the *ifplugd* service in the normal manner for your distribution. That should be it. When you plug in a network cable, be sure to give it about 10 seconds or so before you try to use the card—*ifplugd* needs time to configure the card for your network.

There are also a handful of commands that are particularly useful when troubleshooting your network card. Some of these work with wireless cards as well. I'll assume your wired network card is eth0.

ifconfig

Lists your network interfaces and their settings. Add an actual interface to the command, such as eth0, to see settings specific to that card.

ifconfig *eth0* **up|down**

Activates or deactivates a specific network interface.

dhcpcd *eth0*

Pulls down DHCP configuration information for your network card.

dhcpcd -k *eth0*

Clears the cached DHCP information and sends a signal to the DHCP server to release the IP address.

dhclient *eth0*

Can be used in place of *dhcpcd* in some distributions, such as Mandriva, SUSE, and Ubuntu. This specific command requests configuration information and an IP address lease from a DHCP server.

dhclient -r *eth0*

Releases the DHCP information associated with the card.

Wireless Networking

I'll admit it: when I started this book, I had grand plans of providing configuration information for every form of wireless networking that Linux can support. After several weeks of tinkering and trying configurations on various laptops and distributions, I had to give up. There are just too many variations, and I don't own enough laptops or wireless networking cards to cover them all.

There are several projects that cover the majority of wireless networking possibilities in Linux. Each of these projects exists to handle a particular group of wireless chipsets, with the exception of the last project, which enables you to use nearly any network card that works with Windows. You need to identify the chipset used by your wireless card (you may need to look at your product documentation or perform a web search for your card's model), use that information to find which project drivers support your driver, and either use your distribution's package management tools to install the driver, or visit the project web site and download and compile the drivers yourself. Here is a list of the major wireless driver projects:

linux-wlan-ng

This project has the drivers for the cards based upon the prism2 and 2.5 chipsets, which are the majority of older 802.11b cards from Netgear, Linksys, and many low-end cards. The project site is *http://www.linux-wlan.org*. Here you'll find information about the drivers, how to obtain and install them, and a card matrix that shows you which cards can use these drivers. These drivers work with PCMCIA, USB, and PCI devices.

ipw2100 and ipw2200 (Centrino)

There are drivers to support the wireless technology in the Intel Centrino chipset. There are two main project pages: *http://ipw2100.sourceforge.net* and *http://ipw2200. sourceforge.net*. Many distributions provide packages for these drivers, but you might have to download them through the package management program.

mad-wifi

This project supports cards based on the Atheros chipset, which was one of the earliest chipsets for 802.11a. I've also seen this chipset used for 802.11b/g in Pentium M and Celeron laptops that don't use the Centrino chipset. The project's main web site is *http://madwifi.sourceforge. net*, and you'll find a list of supported cards there.

ndiswrapper

This project, hosted at *http://ndiswrapper.sourceforge.net*, allows you to use Windows wireless drivers to run the card under Linux. It really is an amazing piece of software and a good fallback if there isn't native Linux support for your card, or if you can't figure out how to get it working.

There is more to wireless networking than just getting the card recognized by the operating system. You need to be able to control which network the card connects to, enter encryption key information, and control whether you want to use it at all. If you install the Linux Wireless Tools package for your distribution, you will have access to a few commands that make configuring a WiFi card from the command line quite easy. (Most distributions install this package automatically.) Here are a few basic commands that should prove useful for troubleshooting and making ad hoc changes to your configuration. (I'll assume that your wireless card is eth1 and that these programs, which are often located in */sbin*, are in your path. All configuration commands must be run as root.)

iwconfig

Lists your wireless interfaces and their settings. Add an actual interface, such as eth1, to see settings specific to that card.

iwconfig *eth1* essid *network_name*

Sets the network name to which the network card connects.

iwconfig *eth1* mode *ad-hoc* | *managed*

Sets the operating mode for the card. managed is the most common and requires an access point on the network; ad-hoc can be used for card-to-card networks, but not all cards or drivers support this.

iwconfig *eth1* enc *on* | *off*

Turns wireless encryption on or off. You need to follow this command with the next one to specify the encryption key to be used.

iwconfig *eth1* key s:*password*
> Specifies the WEP encryption key in plain-text form. Alternatively, you can drop s:password and instead enter the hexadecimal value for the key.

iwlist *eth1* scan
> Run this as root to discover which wireless networks are in range of eth1. Not all cards support this function.

In addition to these command-line tools, your distribution might provide configuration tools of its own. Mandrake has such a tool in its control center, as does YaST in SUSE; even Ubuntu provides support in its network control panel.

There are also third-party tools, of which I've found *kwifimanager* the most useful. This should be part of your KDE install, and the configuration screen is found in the KDE Control Center, usually under Internet & Network → Wireless Network. With this tool, you can set configurations for multiple networks, enabling you to roam between locations more easily.

For more information about wireless networking, I suggest you take a look at the information found at *http://www.hpl. hp.com/personal/Jean_Tourrilhes/Linux/*. Although this is a very valuable resource, be careful that you don't end up following instructions from 1999.

X

As explained in the Preface, there are several layers of programs working together in tandem to produce the graphical environment used on a Linux desktop. The base layer (ignoring the work that the kernel and graphic card driver perform) is the X protocol, which handles the display and management of graphical information. Although that sounds like all you need, it isn't. A *window manager* runs on top of X; it handles the actual drawing of the windows on the screen, their appearance, and how the user interacts with them. Some users stop there, but most go on to add a final layer called the *desktop environment*, which provides a set of programs and utilities to unify the desktop and basically try to make the other two layers less obvious. GNOME and KDE are the two most popular desktop environments for Linux.

For now, let's concentrate upon X. Chances are good that when you installed your distribution, X was automatically set up for you. Though these installers do a good job of providing basic X configuration, they often fall short of setting up X exactly the way you want it. For example, widescreen laptops are in widespread use, but they are seldom configured correctly automatically. This section explores some of the more common changes that you will probably want to make to your X configuration.

Most distributions shipping in 2005 and later use the X.org version of X, so I cover that here. However, much of what I write applies equally to the Xfree86 variant—I just haven't tested each step to be sure.

The */etc/X11/xorg.conf* file controls most of the configuration of the X environment. Although a few of the distributions—notably, Fedora, Mandriva, and SUSE—provide graphical tools to deal with the *xorg.conf* file, they are often confusing or provide only limited options. Instead of dealing with those limitations, you should consider working directly with the *xorg.conf* file to achieve fast and reliable results.

You can edit *xorg.conf* using any text editor (make a backup copy first), and changes take effect after you restart the X server. This usually means that you need to log out of your desktop environment, and, from the login manager, select the appropriate option to restart the X server. If you can't find this option, press Ctrl-Alt-Backspace to restart the X server manually. Now, let's move on to the fun stuff—doing useful things.

Creating a Base X Configuration

Some distributions, such as Gentoo, do not create an X configuration file for you; others do a very poor job of it. It is fairly simple to create a basic *xorg.conf* to use as the base for the steps in the following sections. First, you will usually find a commented example file in the */etc/X11* directory. You can copy that as *xorg.conf* and tweak it further for your setup.

However, I usually find it much easier to let X configure itself. To do this, you need to drop out of X completely, which you can do by switching to a virtual console and stopping your display manager (the graphical login screen). To switch to a virtual terminal, press Ctrl-Alt-F1 and log in as root. To stop the display manager, drop to a lower run level with this command:

```
# init 3
```

This command will work in Fedora, Mandriva, and SUSE. When you are ready to get back into X, just run **init 5**. For Gentoo and Ubuntu, you need to stop the display manager instead. Respectively, those commands are:

```
# /etc/init.d/xdm stop          #Gentoo
$ sudo /etc/init.d/gdm stop     #Ubuntu
```

TIP

Ubuntu doesn't allow you to switch to or log in as the root user until you set a password for it: **sudo passwd root**.

When you are ready to run X again, just replace stop with start. With X completely stopped, you are ready to run the configuration program:

```
# X -configure
```

When you run this command, the X system attempts to figure out what hardware you have and create a configuration file to use it. It usually fails in a few regards, such as not detecting the full capabilities of your monitor and not configuring your mouse correctly. The created configuration file is stored as *xorg.conf.new* in your root user's home directory. To make use of this file, copy it to the */etc/X11* directory, name it *xorg.conf*, and launch X manually with the *startx* command.

By default, *startx* will load *twm*, a very basic window manager built into X. To control which desktop environment it loads, create a *.xinitrc* file in your home directory and place the command to start your preferred window manager or desktop environment inside. Chapter 2 has more information about this.

If everything seems to go OK, go ahead and restart your display manager as outlined previously. The most likely error you'll encounter is that X will fail to load because it couldn't detect your mouse. This is easily corrected by editing `xorg.conf` to tell X exactly where to find your mouse. Inside this file, locate the `InputDevice` section for your mouse (it usually has an `Identifier` of `Mouse0`). There is a line labeled `Device`, which you need to change to reflect the actual location of your mouse. The usual paths are: `/dev/input/mice` or `/dev/psaux`. Once you've entered the correct path, try starting X again. The following sections will show you how to configure X the rest of the way.

Setting Resolution and Color Depth

Whether you created your *xorg.conf* yourself or let the distribution do it for you, you'll often find that the screen resolution and color depth are not set at their optimal levels. This is usually caused by two things: the correct driver for your graphic card is not being loaded, or X is not fully aware of your monitor's capabilities.

The first instance is fairly rare with modern distributions and a current version of X. Fixing it is usually rather simple—just look up your graphics card in the Wiki found at *http://wiki.x. org/wiki/VideoDrivers* to get the name of the driver, then insert that name in your *xorg.conf* file in the Device section. For example, if you have a built-in graphic card based upon Intel's 810 chipset, which uses the i810 driver (according to the Wiki), the Device section of your *xorg.conf* file should look similar to this:

```
Section "Device"
     Identifier  "Card0"
     Driver      "i810"
     BusID       "PCI:1:0:0"
```

After you save that change, restart your X server for the change to take effect.

Once you know that the proper graphic driver is being loaded, it is time to tackle your monitor settings—the most likely reason that X is not displaying as you want it to.

There are two sections of your *xorg.conf* file that control what resolution and color depth you can run your monitor at: Monitor and Screen.

Monitor is where you specify the capabilities of your monitor; the values you place here affect the values that will work in the Screen section. Your configuration file should already have the Monitor section set up, but it may be missing or have incorrect values for a couple of options: Horizsync and VertRefresh. The correct values for these options can be obtained from your monitor documentation or by searching on the Web for your monitor model. For example, I have a Samsung Syncmaster 910MP monitor. Performing a web search for this monitor (search string "Syncmaster 910MP specifications"), I quickly found a page that told me the horizontal and vertical scanning frequencies are 31–81 kHz and

56–75 Hz, respectively. Once I input those values in the Monitor section of my *xorg.conf*, it looks like this:

```
Section "Monitor"
        Identifier   "Monitor0"
        VendorName   "Monitor Vendor"
        ModelName    "Monitor Model"
        Horizsync    31-81
        VertRefresh  56-75
```

That's it. With these values specified, X now knows how hard it can drive your monitor, and thus what resolution, color depth, and refresh rate it can support.

Now you need to modify the Screen section to tell X what resolution and color depths you want to use. To do this, you usually need to add a DefaultDepth option and then specify several resolutions to use for that depth. Here is an example of a Screen section, specifying that a monitor should be run at 24-bit color depth and providing options to use resolutions of 1280×768 (typical of widescreen laptop displays) or 640×480:

```
Section "Screen"
   Identifier "Screen0"
   Device     "Card0"
   Monitor    "Monitor0"
      DefaultDepth    24
      SubSection "Display"
         Depth    24
         Modes    "1280x768" "640X480"
      EndSubSection
EndSection
```

Because 1280×768 is specified first, it will be the first resolution X will try to run at. Once you have X running, you can switch between all the available modes by using the *xrandr* program. Run *xrandr* in a terminal window with the –q option to see which resolutions you can run the monitor at. To switch to one of these resolutions, run *xrandr* again with the –s option and specify the resolution like so:

```
$ xrandr -s 640x480
```

KDE provides a graphical tool called *krandrtray* to perform these same transformations. In most distributions, you will find it under K Menu → System with a listing such as Screen Resize & Rotate. When launched, it displays an applet in the system tray. Click on this applet and select a resolution to make a change. There are other ways to get to these settings from within KDE, such as running K Menu → Control Center and choosing Peripherals → Display, or by right-clicking on the desktop and choosing Configure Desktop → Display.

The GNOME tool to change screen resolution is usually found under Desktop → Preferences.

Multiple Mice and Keyboards

As with multiple monitors, X can handle as many input devices as you can physically connect to your computer. Most desktop users will not have more than one mouse or keyboard, but it is not uncommon for laptop owners to use an external mouse and keyboard when they are sitting at a desk.

Multiple keyboards

Getting a second keyboard to work in X is a breeze. Just plug it in. If the keyboard connects to a PS/2 port, you'll need to reboot your computer for it to be recognized. If it connects via USB or a wireless device that plugs into a USB port, then it should be recognized instantly and begin working.

Multiple mice

Configuring a second or third pointer device is a little more complicated. Many laptops come with a trackpad and a trackpoint (the eraser pointer), and you want both to work as well as be able to attach a third external mouse. You'll have to edit your *xorg.conf* file to get this to work, but you're used to that by now.

There are essentially two parts to getting your extra mouse recognized. First, you have to create a new InputDevice section that tells X about your mouse; second, you have to tell X which mouse to pay the most attention to. Here is the text you need to add to your *xorg.conf* file to satisfy the first step:

```
Section "InputDevice"
   Identifier "Mouse2"
   Driver     "mouse"
   Option     "Protocol"    "ExplorerPS/2"
   Option     "Device"  "/dev/input/mice"
   Option     "Emulate3Buttons"   "false"
   Option     "ZAxisMapping"          "4 5"
EndSection
```

You can place this text anywhere, but to keep your configuration file neat, I suggest placing it just after the already configured mouse. From top to bottom, here is what you are telling X about your mouse:

Identifier

> This gives your mouse a user-friendly name. You can use this name to refer to this mouse in other parts of the configuration file.

Driver

> This tells X which driver to use for your mouse—most just use mouse. Graphic tablets and light pens will require other drivers. Touchpads are covered in Chapter 8.

Option "Protocol"

> This tells X how to communicate with your mouse. Except in rare cases, this is the value you see here.

Option "Device"

> This tells X where to physically find your mouse. Most distributions now accept */dev/input/mice* as a generic location for attached USB mice. This is great because it means a single mouse configuration can handle more than one mouse. If your distribution doesn't have this device, you'll need to do some searching to see what your mice are identified as.

Option :Emulate3Buttons

There's not much reason to specify this, as X assumes you won't be emulating three buttons. But, if you give this a true value, X will simulate a middle-button click when you click the left and right buttons at the same time. This is known as *chording*, and it enables you to paste text when you have a mouse with only two buttons.

Option "ZAxisMapping"

This setting configures X so that a scroll wheel will work.

The next step is to tell X which mouse is the core pointer and which is secondary. This step is done in the ServerLayout section, which should be at the top of your *xorg.conf* file. The change to be made is to add a line telling X about your new mouse. Here is a typical ServerLayout with the appropriate line added (in bold):

```
Section "ServerLayout"
   Identifier     "X.org Configured"
   Screen      0  "Screen0" 0 0
   InputDevice    "Mouse1" "CorePointer"
   InputDevice    "Mouse2" "SendCoreEvents"
   InputDevice    "Keyboard0" "CoreKeyboard"
EndSection
```

This line identifies your secondary mouse (Mouse2) and tells it to send its input to the core pointer. If, in the future, you need to add additional mice and the */dev/input/mice* trick doesn't work, you'll need to add a similar InputDevice line for that mouse as well, but be sure to give it a different name.

After any changes to the X configuration file, you need to exit your window manager and restart X (Ctrl-Alt-Backspace) for the changes to take effect.

## CHAPTER 8

Laptops

Many Linux laptop owners treat their machine as if it were nothing more than a portable desktop with an uninterruptible power supply. Their laptops won't sleep, the processor doesn't scale down its speed and consume less power when idle, the LED lights don't light up as they should, and practically none of the extra laptop keys perform their special functions. They use their laptops all the time and love the freedom of movement it gives them, even if that freedom is limited by the measly one-hour battery life they receive.

I can't tell you how many times I've arrived home from work only to find that my laptop battery died during the drive home, or the whole system shut down because the processor got too hot inside the closed bag. This doesn't need to occur because it is possible to get long battery life in Linux, and it is possible to configure the laptop to sleep or hibernate. But Linux laptop configuration is still a bit of kernel, daemon, and script black magic—and it doesn't always work correctly. This chapter is an attempt to give you a grounding in the basics of what is needed and how the pieces fit together. From there, you need to continue the journey online, where up-to-date information can be found.

There are a few valuable online resources to turn to for help configuring your laptop:

http://www.linux-laptop.net
http://www.linux-laptop.org
http://tuxmobil.org

These web sites provide links to hundreds of other web pages where people have detailed the steps they took to get Linux enabled on their specific laptop using a particular distribution. If you're purchasing a laptop with the intention of running Linux on it, visit these sites while researching laptop models to find out which one will work best with Linux.

Touchpads

Let's start with something that's easy to get working. Most distributions do a pretty good job at getting basic touchpad support working. However, none of them tweak the touchpad as far as most people would like. This section will show you how to enable complete support for your Synaptics touchpad (the most common touchpad on laptops) so that you can control mouse speed and sensitivity, create scroll zones, and configure what actions are performed when you tap one, two, or three fingers.

TIP

The other common touchpad is made by Alps. The synaptic drivers covered in this section now include support for Alps touchpads.

Although you will find mouse GUI configuration programs in the various distributions and desktop environments, the settings you change there seldom produce the desired effect upon your touchpad. It is almost always better to manage your touchpad by configuring the */etc/X11/xorg.conf* file.

Before you do this, you need to make sure your distribution is using the actual Synaptic touchpad drivers. If the drivers aren't installed, use your package manager to add them. The package is usually called synaptics, except for Ubuntu, which calls it xorg-driver-synaptics.

Once the package is installed, you have to enable it by adding the appropriate options to your *xorg.conf* file. First, you need to add the option to load the synaptics driver. This is done by adding the following line to your Module section:

```
Load  "synaptics"
```

After that, you need to create a new InputDevice section that specifies what options you want the driver to use. I usually place it right after my existing mouse configuration. Example 8-1 shows a good default configuration that enables most of the features a user would want.

Example 8-1. Sample touchpad configuration

```
Section "InputDevice"
  Driver      "synaptics"
  Identifier  "Mouse1"
  Option      "Device"        "/dev/psaux"
  Option      "Protocol"      "auto-dev"
  Option      "LeftEdge"      "1700"
  Option      "RightEdge"     "5300"
  Option      "TopEdge"       "1700"
  Option      "BottomEdge"    "4200"
  Option      "FingerLow"     "25"
  Option      "FingerHigh"    "30"
  Option      "MaxTapTime"    "180"
  Option      "MaxTapMove"    "220"
  Option      "VertScrollDelta" "100"
  Option      "MinSpeed"      "0.06"
  Option      "MaxSpeed"      "0.12"
  Option      "AccelFactor" "0.0010"
  Option      "CircularScrolling" "1"
  Option      "SHMConfig"     "on"
# Option      "Repeater"      "/dev/ps2mouse"
EndSection
```

Looking at the example, notice the Identifier is Mouse1. What you name it doesn't really matter, as long as it is unique. But, to make sure your touchpad is considered your main pointing device, you need to add, or modify, an option at the top of your configuration file in the ServerLayout section:

```
InputDevice    "Mouse1" "CorePointer"
```

What you name the InputDevice here needs to match what you called it in the InputDevice section from Example 8-1.

You need to log out and restart X (Ctrl-Alt-Backspace) for these changes to take effect. So what do these changes give you?

- Scroll zones along the right and bottom edges of the touchpad. Run your finger along the right side to scroll vertically and along the bottom to scroll horizontally. In Firefox, this motion also moves you through your browser history.

- A single tap on the pad is a left-button click; a tap-release-tap and hold can be used to drag an object; tapping once with two fingers simulates a middle-mouse-button click; and tapping three fingers executes a right-click.

- The CircularScrolling option makes your touchpad like the scroll wheel on an iPod. Visit a long web page and place you finger on the top edge of the touchpad. Move your finger clockwise around the edge to scroll down, and counter-clockwise to scroll up.

If you like GUIs, you can install the KSynaptics package, which adds a Touchpad control panel to your KDE Control Center Peripherals group. Changes made using this control panel take effect as soon as you click Apply or OK.

Kernel Support for Power Management

Laptop power management begins with a properly configured kernel. Fedora, Mandriva, SUSE, and Ubuntu kernels are configured to support Advanced Configuration and Power Interface (ACPI) power management. Gentoo users, who typically build their own kernels, should read the documentation for guidance: *http://www.gentoo.org/doc/en/power-management-guide.xml*.

There is an older standard called Advanced Power Management (APM), but it has fallen out of favor and hasn't really been the standard since about 2002. Many distributions still provide a kernel with APM support, and you may find it a useful fallback for specific functions.

Though some power management support is compiled directly in the kernel, many power options are compiled as loadable kernel modules. Examples of this include support for specific laptop models (like IBM Thinkpads) or the CPU frequency scaling options for specific processors. If your laptop or CPU supports one of these modules, you will need to configure your system to load these modules on boot, using whichever method is preferred by your distribution. In most cases, your distribution is already configured to load these modules as needed. I'll explain more about specific modules in the appropriate sections that come later.

WARNING

A multiprocessor kernel may cause problems for various power management programs. If you are not getting the desired results and are running a uniprocessor system, check to see if your kernel is compiled for SMP with this command: **cat /proc/version**. Recompile your kernel if necessary.

With ACPI support compiled into your kernel, the next step is to run a daemon that will monitor your system for ACPI events. These events are what trigger various scripts that perform the actions necessary to put your system to sleep or hibernate mode. In most distributions, this is called *acpid* and it is enabled by default, or you will find a script for it in your *init* directory. If it is missing, then use your package manager to add it (the package is probably called *acpid* or some variant). Pretty much everything that follows requires this to be running, so do this now.

Extending Battery Life

After you initially install your Linux distribution, you will usually find that your battery life is just awful. Under Windows, your battery probably lasted three to four hours; with Linux, you suddenly get only about one hour of use before the low-power warnings start popping up (if they pop up at all).

Extending your battery life is a multistage process.

Testing Your Battery Life

Linux provides a convenient way to know just how much charge your battery can hold. This is useful information because all the power-saving technology in the world isn't going to double the life of a battery if it is charging to only half of its capacity. Here is the command:

```
$ cat /proc/acpi/battery/BAT0/info |
  grep capacity
design capacity:          47520 mWh
last full capacity:       23220 mWh
design capacity warning:  1161 mWh
design capacity low:      200 mWh
capacity granularity 1:   1 mWh
capacity granularity 2:   1 mWh
```

As you can see, my battery's last fully charged state (last full capacity) is roughly half of its designed capacity. Therefore, I can never expect my laptop battery to last four hours, but I might be able to get two out of it. I wish I had known this before the one-year warranty on the battery expired!

CPU Throttling

The faster your processor runs, the more power it consumes and the hotter it gets, which causes fans to start spinning and use even more power. One technique for configuring a quiet, cool, and low-power laptop is to have Linux slow down your processor when it isn't being used—a technique known as *cpu throttling*. Both Intel SpeedStep and AMD PowerNow! processors can be configured this way.

To achieve throttling, use one of the following programs:

cpudyn

This program responds to the current CPU load to know when to scale things back and save power. It can also be configured to spin down your hard drive, saving a bit more power. The main web site is *http://mnm.uib.es/gallir/cpudyn/*.

cpufreqd

Also known as *cpuspeed*, this daemon responds to CPU load or changes in the battery state (being unplugged). It's a bit more complex to set up than *cpudyn*, but it usually comes with a good default configuration. Visit the web site at *http://sourceforge.net/projects/cpufreqd*, or read the manpage for *cpufreqd.conf* for more information.

powernowd

This small program responds to CPU load and adjusts your CPU speed accordingly. Personally, I found this daemon throttled my CPU more aggressively than the other two, thus saving even more power for me. The project page can be found at *http://www.deater.net/john/powernowd.html*. Don't be fooled by the name—it can also be used with Intel's SpeedStep processors.

To get these programs to work, you must either load these modules or have them compiled into your kernel: *cpufreq_powersave* and *cpufreq_userspace*. In addition, you need to load the module specific to your processor. For a list of module names, list the contents of the directory */lib/modules/kernel_version/kernel/arch/i386/kernel/cpu/cpufreq*. For example, for my IBM T40, I load the module *speedstep-centrino*.

Here is a little trick to see how effective these programs can be (you'll see the fastest change with *powernowd*). Run this command to see the frequency at which your processor is running:

```
$ cat /proc/cpuinfo | grep Mhz
model name      : Intel(R) Pentium(R) M
   processor 1500MHz
cpu MHz         : 1495.548
```

Now, run one of the CPU throttlers. Wait a little bit without doing anything on your laptop, then run the command again. You should see the CPU running at a significantly slower speed. Using *powernowd*, mine drops to 598.219.

If you like the results of the daemon, be sure to set it to start when your computer boots, along with the kernel modules it needs.

Dim or Blank Your Display

The single biggest power consumer on your laptop is your display. You can save power by dimming the display or turning it off when your computer sits idle. When you unplug your AC adapter, your display dims automatically, but probably not to its lowest setting. You should use the keyboard controls for dimming your display to make it as low as possible. Your computer BIOS probably has a setting for a default unplugged level, so you don't have to keep remembering to lower the settings manually.

Blanking your screen is a power management function controlled by X, so it requires some slight adjustments to your *xorg.conf* file. In your Monitor section, enter the following setting:

```
Option    "DPMS"
```

Then, in your ServerLayout section, specify the settings for Display Power Management Signaling (DPMS):

```
# Blank the screen in 10 minutes
Option "BlankTime"    "10"
# Turn off screen in 20 minutes
Option "StandbyTime"    "20"
# Full hibernation in 30 minutes
Option "SuspendTime"    "30"
# Turn off a DPMS aware monitor
Option "OffTime" "40"
```

BlankTime blackens your screen but doesn't turn off the power-hungry backlight; StandbyTime puts the screen in a slightly lower power state; SuspendTime goes even further and saves almost 95 percent power; OffTime turns the monitor off completely. Each time value is expressed in minutes. Obviously, this won't save any power if you are constantly using the system. These settings are useful for desktop systems with CRT displays. LCD panels don't usually have the same hardware features as CRTs, so they don't understand the differences among standby, suspend, and off—each is treated equally and result in the display turning off.

KDE might not honor the settings you put in your X configuration file, so you might want to experiment with the KDE Control Center Peripherals → Display utility to see if it has the desired effects. Also, some distributions may disable DPMS upon system boot. If the commands listed previously don't work for you, this may be your problem. Besides a Google search to see what others have done to solve this issue, you should look at your own */etc/rc.local* file to see whether the "disable DPMS" setting is there.

Power Down Your Hard Drive

Another big power consumer is your hard drive. Data is constantly being read from and written to the drive, which keeps it in a constant state of motion. There are a few things that can be done to help control the situation.

The *cpudyn* program mentioned earlier can spin down your hard drive when it is idle. Read its configuration file for more information. In addition, *hdparm*—a standalone disk utility often used to maximize your drive's performance—can also be used to save power. Here is a basic command that can be used to spin down your hard drive after a period of idleness (you may need to install *hdparm* yourself):

```
# hdparm -S 120
```

This command causes your hard drive to spin down after 10 minutes of idle time. (Each unit in 120 represents 5 seconds.) Most distributions run *hdparm* during bootup to enable DMA and other performance enhancements. Find where the options for this are stored, and you can add your own –S value (try */etc/rc.local*).

However, you'll have only limited success with *hdparm*; Linux just writes to the disk too regularly. If you really want to try to save power by spinning down your disk, you should look into the new "laptop mode." Begin your search here: *http://www.linuxjournal.com/article/7539*.

Putting Your Laptop to Sleep

There are basically two low-power modes you can put your laptop into: sleep and hibernation. When you put your laptop to *sleep*, it spins down the hard drive, shuts off the monitor, and cuts power to the CPU. At this point, your laptop just needs to expend power to keep the memory refreshed, because this is where your current data is stored. This is why sleep mode is often called *suspend to RAM*.

Once you close your laptop's lid, it goes to sleep within just a few seconds, and it usually takes just four or five seconds for it to come out of sleep. Sleep is the most useful form of laptop "suspension," and it is the dream of Linux laptop users to achieve it. Unfortunately, not many do. Sleep is perhaps one of the hardest things for a Linux user to configure his system to use reliably.

The best way to get sleep working for your laptop is to copy the steps someone else performed with the same or similar model laptop. The web sites at the beginning of this chapter provide listings of hundreds of setups for a wide variety of models. Search these sites to find out how someone else configured the hardware on their laptop. You won't find success in all these instances, but after reading, you'll have a better understanding of what is achievable with your own laptop.

Sleep basically comes down to getting your system to recognize that a power management event has occurred and then execute a set of commands based upon that event. For sleep, the key events are the opening and closing of the laptop lid. For this to work, you need to have a few things configured:

- Support for ACPI power management in your kernel.
- If available, support for your laptop model in the kernel or compiled as a module.
- The *acpid* power management daemon.
- Scripts that recognize the power management events and perform an action.

The *acpid* scripts are usually located in */etc/acpi/events* and */etc/acpi/actions*. Your distribution might already have some scripts located there. With my IBM T40 and other laptops, I've used the scripts located at *http://www.thinkwiki.org/wiki/How_to_configure_acpid* with great success. Don't forget to make the "action" script executable. If you find that these scripts aren't working for you, then you might want to continue to search for ACPI scripts that apply to your laptop brand or model. Don't forget about the resources introduced at the beginning of this chapter.

Sleep doesn't always work reliably on any model of laptop, and on some models it is very flaky. Common problems include:

- The laptop never wakes up and is unresponsive to any keyboard input, requiring you to power down the laptop.

- The display doesn't come back up, requiring you to kill X (Ctrl-Alt-Backspace). Sometimes the display just looks funny until you launch a program or switch virtual desktops. To overcome this, many sleep scripts switch to a virtual console before going to sleep.

- The sound or your network interface may not wake up, requiring you to configure it manually. For this reason, many sleep scripts unload the modules running these devices before going to sleep, then load them when the laptop wakes.

- The touchpad may lose the ability to respond to taps until X is restarted.

Hibernating Your Laptop

Hibernation is more than just a deep form of sleep. With hibernation, also known as *suspend to disk*, all the contents of memory are saved to the hard disk and then the laptop shuts off, completely. When the laptop comes out of hibernation, instead of going through a lengthy boot process, it instead reads the contents of memory from the hard drive and returns to exactly the state at which you put the laptop into hibernation. This usually cuts 20 or more seconds out of the boot process, and it means that you don't have to relaunch any programs. Hibernation works in Linux much better than sleep does—too bad it isn't as convenient to use.

Your best bet for getting hibernation to work reliably is to use the kernel patch and hibernate script found at *http://www.suspend2.net*. You'll need to follow the steps outlined at the web site to get this going. To summarize:

1. Download the kernel sources for your system and patch with the software-suspend patch for your kernel version.

2. Compile a custom kernel with Software Suspend 2 compiled in. Don't confuse this with Software Suspend, which may already be in your kernel. Reboot with the new kernel.

3. Download and install the hibernate script.

4. Test from a console first with X completely shut down. This usually means switching to a virtual console (Ctrl-Alt-F1) and going to a non-GUI runlevel (usually init3 as root; check Chapter 2 for specifics). If this works, try it again under X.

Before you mess around with suspend to disk, I highly suggest you make a backup of your data files. This power management mode is still experimental, and you should confirm its reliability for your setup before entrusting it with your data.

Distribution Support

Each of the distributions covered in this book already partially takes you down the path to laptop nirvana; however, not one of them makes it the whole way. What follows is a very quick breakdown of the default power management support each distribution gives you, so you have a better understanding of where to begin in your pursuit of the perfect laptop experience.

Fedora

Because it's a major distribution, I find it surprising that Fedora has very little configured by default with regard to power management. Out of the box, the Fedora kernel supports ACPI and APM, and daemons are run upon boot to make these services available to the user, but other than running *cpuspeed* to throttle your processor, nothing else is done.

There are no ACPI event and action scripts, no hibernation support, and no control panels for configuring your power management. This means that you have a very clean slate to start with, and most of the advice given previously should apply to you.

Gentoo

Out of the box, Gentoo doesn't come configured to do anything special to make your laptop experience better. That is just the nature of the distribution—it is for do-it-yourselfers. The generic advice given in this chapter for power management particularly applies to Gentoo, as you are starting from scratch and don't have any "partial" solutions to have to work around.

The best advice I can give you is to look at the web sites listed at the beginning of this chapter and look for any write-ups about your laptop that focus on Gentoo. Also, read the Gentoo documentation for power management: *http://www.gentoo.org/doc/en/power-management-guide.xml*. Following the advice on this web page, and other suggestions found in the Gentoo forums, I've had more success with configuring my laptop (and IBM T40) on Gentoo than any of the other distributions covered here (Ubuntu was a close second). It really came down to the quality of the documentation more than the actual abilities of the distribution.

Mandriva

Mandriva doesn't provide any centralized control panels to configure your laptop's power management features. However, it does come configured with APM and ACPI support, the appropriate modules for CPU speed control, and a script to suspend to disk.

This script is called *pmsuspend2*, and it can be run directly by the user. If you feel so inclined, you can piece together instructions to assign this script to the action of closing your laptop lid or pressing a key combination, such as one of the function keys.

SUSE

None of the other distributions I've used has done as much to make laptop use convenient as SUSE has. It comes with kernel support for both APM and ACPI, and provides its own power management daemon called *powersave*. This package supports ACPI, APM, hard drive spin down, and processor throttling (both PowerNow! and SpeedStep). While running the *powersave* daemon, you should not run *apmd*, *acpid*, *ospmd*, or *cpufreqd* (*cpuspeed*) as the functions of each of these programs have been incorporated into *powersave*.

To control your laptop settings, open YaST, click the System icon, then select Power Management. In this control program, you'll find a set of schemes for AC and Battery power, as well as settings to configure ACPI events (pressing the power or sleep buttons, as well as closing the laptop lid), what actions to perform when the battery power is low, and which modes of suspend to enable (suspend to disk or to RAM). In my experiments, this has all worked rather well, with the exception of sleep (which is disabled by default). This desired suspension mode continues to cause problems for some laptop models, even for a distribution that has obviously spent time trying to solve the problem.

Ubuntu

One reason I like Ubuntu is its laserlike focus upon the issues that matter most to desktop Linux users. And though Ubuntu doesn't quite have all features or control panels that SUSE has, it has not ignored laptop power management and has provided several nice ACPI scripts to help you get sleep and hibernate working. Like the other distributions, its kernel also comes precompiled to support CPU throttling, and *powernowd* is already configured to run on boot.

To enable sleep, edit the configuration file found at */etc/default/acpi-support*, and uncomment the line `# ACPI_SLEEP=true`. You'll find additional settings in this file and you should look through it to see if there is anything else of interest. For example, some hardware won't be reinitialized when your laptop wakes up, but you can try to work around this by using the `MODULES` config line to unload then reload kernel modules. You need to restart *acpid* after you make changes to this file:

```
$ sudo /etc/init.d/acpid
```

Hibernation is configured by default. The option to do this is on the logout dialog. When you resume (by pressing the power button), you'll come back to the state you were in before you chose the hibernate option, with all programs running.

In addition to the other laptop web sites I've mentioned, you should look at the Ubuntu Laptop Wiki page: *https://wiki.ubuntu.com/HardwareSupportMachinesLaptops*. Many Ubuntu users are posting their solutions to laptop issues on this Wiki.

Running Commands and Editing Text

Throughout this book, I've asked you to edit text files and enter commands at a shell prompt. Using these methods probably seems archaic to Windows and Mac users or those new to Linux. But the truth is that using the command line and editing configuration files is simply the way Linux works. Many of these tasks are less intuitive than using a GUI configuration program, but that doesn't mean they are not legitimate ways to configure a system. It's not like typing a command is all that difficult, and once you know what you are doing, it is a fast and efficient way to perform tasks and configure your system.

Some readers of this book might not feel comfortable with these tasks yet. This appendix is a very brief introduction to using the command line and editing text files. My purpose here is merely to teach you enough to perform the steps I give in this book. If you want to master these topics, you should read any one of the dozen books on the subjects, such as O'Reilly's *Linux Pocket Guide*, *Learning the Bash Shell*, and *Learning the vi Editor*.

Using the Command Line

Working at the command line is not particularly difficult. The real problem is knowing what to type and avoiding typos. This book shows you what to type—and practice should help reduce typos.

To work at the command line, you need a terminal emulator. Both GNOME and KDE provide one. GNOME's is called *gnome-terminal*, and you can get to it from Applications → System Tools → Terminal, or just type **gnome-terminal** in the run dialog (Alt-F2). KDE's is called *Konsole*, and you can launch it from K Menu → System → Konsole, but if you can't find it, just enter **konsole** in a run dialog (Alt-F2).

Either way, you'll end up with a window that displays a command prompt. This is where you type in your commands. At the minimum, a command consists of a program name, but that can also be followed by one or more options and arguments. An option is an additional feature of the command, and an argument tells the command what to act upon. On this line, the dollar sign ($) is the command prompt:

```
$ command option(s) argument(s)
```

After you type in the text, press Enter to execute. Here's an example:

```
$ more -p /etc/fstab
```

The command is *more*, which displays the text in a file one screenful at a time. The option is –p, which tells *more* to clear the screen before displaying the text of the file. And the argument is */etc/fstab*, which tells *more* which file to read.

WARNING

Commands are case-sensitive, so you must type them exactly as you see them in this book.

You can edit commands that you've typed. Using the left and right arrows, you can move forward and backward in the text and use the Backspace key to delete any errors. If you run a command with a typo in it, you'll usually receive an error. To correct the command and run it again, press the up arrow once and you'll see the command you just entered—then you can edit it and run again. Each time you press the up arrow, you'll go one command further back in your command history.

You will occasionally need to run commands with higher permissions than are assigned to you, the current user. This usually means running them as the superuser root. To elevate your user privileges, use the following command:

```
$ su -
Password: ********
#
```

WARNING

The root user has complete control over the system. With a wrong command, it is possible for you to delete all of your files, cause your machine to crash, or render your system completely unusable. When you are done performing your task as root, change back to your normal user by typing **exit** at the prompt.

You'll need to enter the root password for your system (when you installed Linux, you should have been asked to create this). Note that the prompt changes from $ to #. Even if your prompt has other text, it will almost always end with one of these characters. The first prompt type ($) indicates a normal user; the second (#) indicates root. With the commands in this book, each time you see the # sign, you need to make sure you are logged in as root before running them. When you are done running commands as root, log out by typing **exit** at the prompt.

By default, Ubuntu does not allow you to switch to the root user. Instead, it configures a program called *sudo* that you can use to elevate your privileges as needed. *sudo* can be configured for other distributions as well, but that is beyond the scope of this appendix. Here is a sample command using *sudo*:

```
$ sudo vi /etc/fstab
Password: ********
```

The password you type is the one for your user. You'll need to repeat the *sudo* command each time you run a command as root in this way. However, within a time window of about five minutes, you won't have to type your password again.

When you're done using the command line, you can close the terminal by typing **exit**.

Editing Text Files

Text editing is pretty simple. You'll usually do this from the command line because most configuration files need to be modified as the root user, and the easiest way to do that is from the terminal.

Every Linux user has his favorite text editor, but I'm going to cover only the one that is almost guaranteed to be on every Linux and Unix machine you'll encounter: *vi*.

When you launch *vi*, you need to tell it which file you want to edit. If the file is in your current directory, you can just type in the name, but if it is another directory, type in the path to the file and the name. Whenever I ask you to edit a text file, I either give you the exact path or tell you where the file is. For example, to edit the configuration file for X that is found in */etc/X11/*, you would type the following command:

```
$ sudo vi /etc/X11/xorg.conf
```

As you can see, I used the *sudo* command to run this editing session as root.

Once you're in *vi*, there are a few things you need to know. First, *vi* has a command mode and an insert mode. You are in command mode by default. While in this mode, you can move your insertion cursor around and execute commands (such as ones to save the file or delete lines).

Use your arrow keys to move your cursor around while in command mode. Once your cursor is where it needs to be for an edit, press **i** to enter insert mode. Make your edits, then press **Esc** to go back to command mode. Repeat as often as necessary.

When you are done making changes, make sure you are in command mode by pressing **Esc**, then type **:wq** to save the file. These keys are pressed in order, not at the same time. An alternative command is **ZZ** (both capitalized and without a colon). If you don't want to save your changes, type **:q!** instead. Table A-1 lists a few more commands you might be interested in. Remember: these commands are used while in command mode only.

Table A-1. vi editor commands

Command	Result
I	Enters insert mode.
A	Moves cursor to the end of the line and enters insert mode.
o	Enters insert mode one line below the current one; this adds an additional line.
x	Deletes the highlighted character.
Esc	Exits insert mode and returns to command mode.
ZZ	Exits and saves the current document.
:wq	Exits and saves the current document.
:q!	Exits the current document without saving.
/	Searches for the string you enter afterwards.
n	Repeats the search you just performed with /.
Arrow keys	Moves around a document one character or line at a time.
PgUp, PgDn	Moves around a document one page at a time.

While in command mode, you can search the file, which helps you find the text to change in a long configuration file. To do this, type a forward slash /. At the bottom of the screen, the forward slash will appear and you can type in your search criteria, then press Enter to start the search. Press **n** to repeat the search if the first results weren't the actual text you were looking for.

There is a lot more *vi* can do, and power users will groan at this simple summary. Nonetheless, this information should be sufficient to enable you to edit the text files as required by this book.

Index

We'd like to hear your suggestions for improving our indexes. Send email to
index@oreilly.com.

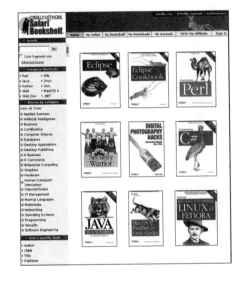

Related Titles from O'Reilly

Linux

Building Embedded Linux Systems

Building Secure Servers with Linux

The Complete FreeBSD, *4th Edition*

Even Grues Get Full

Exploring the JDS Linux Desktop

Extreme Programming Pocket Guide

GDB Pocket Reference

Knoppix Hacks

Knoppix Pocket Guide

Learning Red Hat Enterprise Linux and Fedora, *4th Edition*

Linux Cookbook

Linux Desktop Hacks

Linux Device Drivers, *3rd Edition*

Linux in a Nutshell, *5th Edition*

Linux in a Windows World

Linux iptables Pocket Reference

Linux Network Administrator's Guide, *3rd Edition*

Linux Pocket Guide

Linux Security Cookbook

Linux Server Hacks

Linux Unwired

Linux Web Server CD Bookshelf, *Version 2.0*

LPI Linux Certification in a Nutshell

Managing RAID on Linux

More Linux Server Hacks

OpenOffice.org Writer

Programming with Qt, *2nd Edition*

Root of all Evil

Running Linux, *5th Edition*

Samba Pocket Reference, *2nd Edition*

Test Driving Linux

Understanding the Linux Kernel, *3rd Edition*

Understanding Open Source & Free Software Licensing

User Friendly

Using Samba, *2nd Edition*

Version Control with Subversion

O'REILLY®

Keep in touch with O'Reilly

1. Download examples from our books

To find example files for a book, go to:
www.oreilly.com/catalog

select the book, and follow the "Examples" link.

2. Register your O'Reilly books

Register your book at *register.oreilly.com*

Why register your books? Once you've registered your O'Reilly books you can:

- Win O'Reilly books, T-shirts or discount coupons in our monthly drawing.
- Get special offers available only to registered O'Reilly customers.
- Get catalogs announcing new books (US and UK only).
- Get email notification of new editions of the O'Reilly books you own.

3. Join our email lists

Sign up to get topic-specific email announcements of new books and conferences, special offers, and O'Reilly Network technology newsletters at:
elists.oreilly.com

It's easy to customize your free elists subscription so you'll get exactly the O'Reilly news you want.

4. Get the latest news, tips, and tools
www.oreilly.com

- "Top 100 Sites on the Web"—PC Magazine
- CIO Magazine's Web Business 50 Awards

Our web site contains a library of comprehensive product information (including book excerpts and tables of contents), downloadable software, background articles, interviews with technology leaders, links to relevant sites, book cover art, and more.

5. Work for O'Reilly

Check out our web site for current employment opportunities:
jobs.oreilly.com

6. Contact us

O'Reilly & Associates
1005 Gravenstein Hwy North
Sebastopol, CA 95472 USA

TEL: 707-827-7000 or 800-998-9938
(6am to 5pm PST)

FAX: 707-829-0104

order@oreilly.com
For answers to problems regarding your order or our products.
To place a book order online, visit:
www.oreilly.com/order_new

catalog@oreilly.com
To request a copy of our latest catalog.

booktech@oreilly.com
For book content technical questions or corrections.

corporate@oreilly.com
For educational, library, government, and corporate sales.

proposals@oreilly.com
To submit new book proposals to our editors and product managers.

international@oreilly.com
For information about our international distributors or translation queries. For a list of our distributors outside of North America check out:
international.oreilly.com/distributors.html

adoption@oreilly.com
For information about academic use of O'Reilly books, visit:
academic.oreilly.com

O'REILLY®